T0220733

DBA Survivor

Become a Rock Star DBA

Thomas LaRock

Apress®

DBA Survivor: Become a Rock Star DBA

Copyright © 2010 by Thomas LaRock

All rights reserved. No part of this work may be reproduced or transmitted in any form or by any means, electronic or mechanical, including photocopying, recording, or by any information storage or retrieval system, without the prior written permission of the copyright owner and the publisher.

ISBN-13 (pbk): 978-1-4302-2787-8

ISBN-13 (electronic): 978-1-4302-2788-5

Trademarked names may appear in this book. Rather than use a trademark symbol with every occurrence of a trademarked name, we use the names only in an editorial fashion and to the benefit of the trademark owner, with no intention of infringement of the trademark.

President and Publisher: Paul Manning
Lead Editor: Jonathan Gennick
Technical Reviewers: Sylvester Carstarphen, Darl Kuhn, Michele LaRock, Brent Ozar, Michael Russo, Ken Simmons, Jared Still
Editorial Board: Clay Andres, Steve Anglin, Mark Beckner, Ewan Buckingham, Tony Campbell, Gary Cornell, Jonathan Gennick, Jonathan Hassell, Michelle Lowman, Matthew Moodie, Jeffrey Pepper, Frank Pohlmann, Ben Renow-Clarke, Dominic Shakeshaft, Matt Wade, Tom Welsh
Coordinating Editor: Laurin Becker
Copy Editor: Damon Larson, Katie Stence
Compositor: MacPS, LLC
Indexer: John Collin
Artist: April Milne

Distributed to the book trade worldwide by Springer-Verlag New York, Inc., 233 Spring Street, 6th Floor, New York, NY 10013. Phone 1-800-SPRINGER, fax 201-348-4505, e-mail orders-ny@springer-sbm.com, or visit www.springeronline.com.

For information on translations, please e-mail rights@apress.com, or visit www.apress.com.

Apress and friends of ED books may be purchased in bulk for academic, corporate, or promotional use. eBook versions and licenses are also available for most titles. For more information, reference our Special Bulk Sales–eBook Licensing web page at www.apress.com/info/bulksales.

The information in this book is distributed on an "as is" basis, without warranty. Although every precaution has been taken in the preparation of this work, neither the author(s) nor Apress shall have any liability to any person or entity with respect to any loss or damage caused or alleged to be caused directly or indirectly by the information contained in this work.

For Suzanne, Isabelle, and Elliot. Thank you for sharing your lives with mine.

Contents at a Glance

Contents

Foreword

You hold in your hands a collection of insight and wisdom on the topic of database administration gained through many years of hard-won experience, long nights of study, and direct mentorship under some of the industry's most talented database professionals and information technology (IT) experts.

Consider the standard university approach to training people in our discipline. Many colleges and universities offer a curriculum in "computer science," encouraging their alumni with lucrative careers in "software engineering." Yet, anyone who's spent much time working with computer technology will tell you that these terms are often misleading. After all, any type of science is predicated upon the Scientific Method: characterize your observations and experiences, construct a hypothesis, predict a logical deduction, and test the hypothesis and prediction using one or more experiments. Does that sound like what information technologists and computer programmers do? Not just "no," but "Heck No!" While it is certainly true that some computer technologists experiment (usually in the fields of processor design, networking technology design, security and encryption algorithms, and certain fundamental software technology platforms) this might represent 0.02 percent of the total information technology workforce around the world and frequently requires a doctoral degree.

Going a step further, let's look at the term "software engineer." While a full definition of the term "engineer" could fill a couple of paragraphs, the connation of the word implies the application of knowledge in science and mathematics to solve a problem with predictable results whose operation and outcome can be reliably forecast. Engineers take their profession seriously and rest their credibility on producing designs that perform as expected without causing unintended harm to the public at large. Does that sound a lot like what you do? Does that sound like the jobs of anyone you know who work with IT?

It doesn't sound like any IT professionals I know. While the IT profession has made many strides over the years and has greatly improved their ability to produce predictable results and reduce unintended consequences, we're still subjected to daily hot fixes, software patches, and countless interruptions that disqualify computer programming and IT from consideration as both a science and an engineering discipline.

Instead, I offer an alternative interpretation of our chosen career path. When we look at the scope of human undertaking, we can see many careers and disciplines that closely mimic our experiences as IT professionals (or IT professional wannabees). But the closest matches aren't in the computer field, they're in the creative arts. Don't believe me? Consider this comparison. Engineers and scientists need to completely and deeply understand the minutia of their discipline. A good friend of mine is literally a rocket scientist working for NASA and possesses an encyclopedic knowledge of metrology (used in the rocketry structures) and chemistry (used in the rocket fuels). That's not what we need. When was the last time you talked to a database administrator (DBA) who had exhaustive knowledge of the hashing algorithms used to buffer data into and out of the system RAM of their chosen database platform? Instead, we need to know computational algorithms about as much as a sculptor needs to know the molecular crystalline structure of marble and quartz or a musician needs to understand the science of acoustic resonance. When was the last time a musician sat you down to discuss the effect of humidity and altitude upon their next performance? (Perhaps not ironically, many IT professionals are also part-time musicians.)

Musicians need to know a heck of a lot more than acoustics, and sculptors need to know a lot more than geology. The people in the creative arts are makers, and by choosing the path of DBA, you'll be one too. One extremely important lesson we can take from makers is that they learn best in two ways. First, makers learn by constant practice and hands-on tinkering. You will need to do this too to become truly good at database administration. When you conjure an image of an "inventor," you probably envision a guy with messy hair, a white lab coat, and a harried-looking laboratory. Guess what? All good DBAs I know do indeed have a lab, usually called the dev environment. That's where they regularly tinker and experiment and test.

My second and most important comparison to other makers is that they need at least one good mentor to launch their career. Every maker's education includes years of lessons at the feet of others who were more advanced than them, whether they are artist, musician, or yes, DBA. That's where this book comes into play. You might not have a senior DBA to lean on for advice and inspiration, but you have one in this book. Many of the fundamental lessons for a new database administrator, as a review of this book's table of contents quickly reveals, are about how you interact with other people in your enterprise's IT environment. Yes, it's very important to know the technology, and you'll learn a great deal about technology by reading this book and applying its lessons. However, you'll also learn about the relationships between DBAs and software developers and corporate managers—areas where you must be guarded and areas where you must be hardnosed.

Of course, no single book can ever teach you everything you need to know about a discipline as broad and far-reaching as database administration for Microsoft SQL Server. So Tom has taken pains to show you the first steps. He gives sources for additional learning, ways of finding a mentor, and—when the time comes—a means of you becoming a mentor yourself. I exhort you to make the most of this fine book and, when you're ready, take the lessons you've learned and give them back to the SQL Server community.

Kevin Kline

Technical Strategy Manager, Quest Software

Founding board member of PASS, the Professional Association for SQL Server

In very "real" language, you hold a book in your hands that will help you understand the day-to-day life of the Database Administrator. From how you become a database administrator, to backups and recover, and, of course, the joys of bacon—it's all here. (OK, a word about that last sentence. Thomas likes bacon. A lot. In fact, he believes that just about anything is better with bacon, so it follows that you'll get a mention or two on it in any book he writes.)

Other than the bacon information, Thomas lays out his real world experience with database systems. You'll learn how to work in a development team, and not to fear outsourcing. You'll find out how to maintain a production system, and how to monitor the systems under control. Thomas even explains how to leverage the SQL Server community to help you, and how you can help them back.

So if you've got an evening or two to kill, and you're thinking about becoming a DBA, welcome aboard. You're in for a treat.

Buck Woody

Senior Technology Specialist, Microsoft

About the Author

 **Thomas LaRock** is a seasoned IT professional with over a decade of technical and management experience. Currently serving as a database administration manager with a financial services company, Thomas has progressed through several roles including programmer, analyst, and DBA. Prior to being a DBA, he worked at several software and consulting companies at customer sites in the United States and abroad. Thomas holds a MS degree in Mathematics from Washington State University, is a member of Quest Software's Association of SQL Server Experts, currently serves on the Board of Directors for the Professional Association for SQL Server (PASS), and is a SQL Server MVP.

About the Technical Reviewers

Sylvester Carstarphen is a working DBA manager at a leading automobile CRM company, where he is passionate about developing his team's soft skills as well as their DBA skills. Sylvester has been a DBA for 6+ plus years with strong performance tuning skills. He is also the co-author of Pro SQL Server 2008 Administration by Apress.

Darl Kuhn has been an Oracle DBA since 1992. For the past 14 years, he has been a volunteer DBA for the Rocky Mountain Oracle Users Group. Darl also teaches Oracle classes at Regis University in the department of computer information technology.

Michele LaRock MS RD LDN is a Registered Dietitian with a Masters degree from Bastyr University in Seattle. When not providing her brother with nutritional advice about Turbaconduckens, she counsels others in Holistic Nutrition, including her husband and two children.

Brent Ozar is a Microsoft MVP and a SQL Server Expert for Quest Software. He has over a decade of broad IT experience, performing SQL Server database administration, systems administration, SAN administration, virtualization administration, and project management. He has spoken around the globe at events for PASS, SQLBits, SSWUG, and other organizations. Brent founded the Virtualization Virtual Chapter for the Professional Association for SQL Server (PASS), and serves as the Editor-in-Chief at SQLServerPedia.com.

Michael Russo is a former student athletic trainer at the University of New Hampshire and is a frequent jogging partner for Thomas LaRock. When not dragging Tom through the streets or to a track at lunchtime, he often reminds Tom about good nutritional choices and has slapped a donut from Tom's hand on more than one occasion.

Ken Simmons is a database administrator, developer, and Microsoft SQL Server MVP. He is the Author of Pro SQL Server 2008 Administration (Apress, 2009), Pro SQL Server 2008 Mirroring (Apress, 2009), and Pro SQL Server 2008 Policy-Based Management (Apress, 2010). He has been working in the IT industry since 2000 and currently holds certifications for MCP, MCAD, MCSD, MCDBA, and MCTS for SQL 2005.

Jared Still, Certifiable Oracle DBA and Part Time Perl Evangelist, has been a DBA for quite a few years now, but tries to keep that dyed-in-the-wool status from hindering his progress by continuing to learn about databases and computer systems in general. And yes, he really is a Part Time Perl Evangelist.

Acknowledgments

A lot of people helped me to produce this book. The words contained in these pages represent my journey over the past ten years. But there were many influences prior to that as well.

To my wife Suzanne, thank you for your love and patience.

To my children, Isabelle and Elliot, thank you for always finding a way to make me smile.

To my parents, thanks for everything.

To Chris and Sally, thanks for helping me get started on my path.

To Vinny and Craig, thanks for believing I could be a DBA.

To Frank, thanks for helping me understand what it means to be a DBA.

To Lori, Sean, Joe, Andre, and Pankaj thanks for being such a wonderful team.

To my technical editors, thank you for reviewing my words and helping me stay on track.

To my editor, Jonathan, thank you for believing in this book.

Introduction

Congratulations! You have accepted a position as a Database Administrator. What's that? Oh, you were *told* that you were going to be the new DBA? No worries, I am certain you were carefully selected to be the best…of the best…of the best. Now that you have the job, what's next? What is your action plan? What do you take care of first? Who should you look to make friends with, and fast? And how much more will you get paid?

First off, let's get some basics out of the way. You do not know everything. Sorry to tell you, but better to find out now rather than later on. Trust me. No one person knows everything; it is a fact of human existence. You are human, right? Because that simple fact will be questioned periodically, so you better check again just to make certain. Last thing you want is to find out you are actually a Cylon or something worse.

Another thing you need to know about being a DBA is that you will have fewer friends at work than when you started. Now, that is not necessarily a bad thing. See, you have been placed into a position of responsibility, and with this responsibility you will need to make some decisions, and those decisions will not always be popular. Thus, you may lose some friends at work, but these losses will be more than offset by the gains you have in the overall DBA community. So you have that going for you, which is nice.

With that responsibility, you will also find that you start getting more blame than credit for your work. I promise you this: no one will ever stop by your desk in the morning and thank you for the fact that everything ran smoothly last night. But you better believe if a batch load took five minutes longer than expected, you will have four different people asking you "WTF?"

While being a DBA may not be all unicorns and rainbows, it has the potential to be the most rewarding career path you could ever be presented with. Ask around and you will find that most people cherish having a good DBA on hand. It is my hope that this book will give you the tools necessary to be that DBA—the one they decide they cannot live without.

Chapter 1

How Did I Get Here?

Database administration is one of those professions that makes it hard to explain to others what you do for a living. We typically fit in between the people who build servers and the people who need to store and retrieve data from those same servers. We are therefore expected to know and understand a lot about a lot, and it can be overwhelming at times. So much so that you will sometimes stop to take a moment to reflect upon where you are in life and wonder, "How did I get here?"

I am often asked two questions. The first is, "How did you become a DBA?" The second question is, "What does a DBA do, exactly?" This chapter will help to explain the former, and the remaining chapters will help to explain the latter. Becoming a DBA can be a mysterious journey for most. I will share with you my story and the stories of others in an effort to help you better understand how some people end up becoming DBAs.

> **TIP:** Be careful what you wish for, because you might just get it.

In this chapter, we will discuss the following:

1. My journey
2. Other journeys
3. Your journey
4. Staying focused

My Journey

How did I become a DBA? It sure wasn't the career I dreamed of in elementary school. I probably wanted to be a fireman or a policeman back then.

I can't say that I planned to become a DBA either, at least not at first, not early in my career. My entry into the DBA world sort of just happened. Some might see it as "dumb luck," but I prefer the term "smart luck."

Early Lessons

My first computer? That would be the Commodore VIC-20. I remember saving my money from mowing lawns, my sister driving me to the mall, and buying that all-in-one unit that I could attach to my television with an RF adapter. I also got the datasette, which was nothing more than a cassette tape player, but it allowed me to save programs, which was nice.

I bought a book of programs that I could type myself and run. Did you know that sometimes books have mistakes printed in them? Imagine a computer program in a book that was missing a couple of important characters. I didn't have to imagine such a thing, because I lived it. I would often find myself debugging programs. To this day, I believe that is the biggest reason I do iterative debugging; I always make small changes and measure the effects as I progress, whereas others like to do a lot of work and try to debug everything afterward.

In addition to being drawn toward computers at an early age, I was also drawn toward mathematics. Both of those fields are analytical in nature and served as a good base for me later in life. Oh, and neither field required me to do a lot of writing, which was nice as well. In fact, I went to college as a math major just to keep the number of term papers to a minimum.

> **TIP:** Going the extra mile and doing a little extra work always pays off in the long run.

Unfortunately, my lack of writing experience caught up with me in graduate school. In my very first class there, the professor told me I needed to write out my solutions; I needed to write out the word *two* instead of using the numerical 2. And I could not just use =; I had to write *equals*. It was a painful adjustment for me, but it served me well. By that time in my life, I had learned that the path less traveled usually led me to a better place than I would have imagined.

While in graduate school, I had the option of composing a master's project as part of earning my degree. Since knowing how doing extra work had always paid off for me in the past, I decided to take on a project. The math and astronomy departments at Washington State University (WSU) were joined at the time, and I had a natural love for all things extraterrestrial (and still do). I asked one of the astronomy professors if he would work with me on a project and he agreed.

My project was titled "The Interstellar Radiation Field of Globular Clusters" and involved quite a bit of programming. Not Commodore VIC-20 programming; we are talking FORTRAN77, Sun boxes, astrophysical equations, arrays, telescopes, charts, graphs, and even LaTeX. I was exposed to a lot of programming in a very short time, and left WSU with a master of science (MS) in mathematics and enough programming experience to help me land a job.

Early Career

I left graduate school with my MS in hand as I felt that would give me more opportunities to find work than if I continued on to get a PhD. I found myself in an interview one day with a man who had a PhD in physics. We spent most of my interview talking about the project I had done at WSU. He needed someone to do some programming work with PowerBuilder. I still remember his remark to me: "I can teach you whatever I need you to do and I know you'll be able to do the work."

And with that, I was hired. As a PowerBuilder developer. With no experience in PowerBuilder.

I was there for about a year and a half, and then I jumped to a software company that was also looking for some PowerBuilder help. Of course, by then I actually had some PowerBuilder experience. But what I still did not have was any real database experience. All I knew was that my data went somewhere and it came back when I needed it. I did pick up a few things there with regard to database design, triggers, stored procedures, and a realization that I was interested in learning more.

After another year, I found myself at a new company that was looking for some PowerBuilder help. I took the job, and after about a year or so there, I came to realize two things. First, I needed to do something other than PowerBuilder because there was going to come a day when PowerBuilder would not be in enough of a demand for me to keep finding work. Second, I wanted to become a DBA.

> **TIP:** Find something in life that you have a passion for; it makes other life decisions easy.

I looked upon the role of a DBA as one that does not disappear in the same way as a developer who knows only one particular language. To that point, I had done mostly PowerBuilder work and had just started getting involved in .NET. The idea of having to learn a new language every few years in order to stay marketable seemed daunting at the time. But to be a DBA meant I would be the "man behind the curtain," always turning knobs and always being able to find work.

So I sought out opportunities to help out with DBA tasks. And when my company looked to bring on a full-time DBA, I went to the hiring manager with my résumé. She promptly told me that they would not think to hire me for the job because I had no experience. Instead, they were going to bring in someone they had worked with before. I felt disappointed for about thirty seconds and then the manager told me that they would also be looking to start up a "junior DBA" program to train people to help out in times of need. She wanted to put my name down as a person interested in attending the in-house training, and I agreed.

THE SHADOW KNOWS!

by Brent Ozar

If you want to become a DBA, and your company won't send you for training, ask if they'll let you shadow the company's DBA for one day per week. If they don't go for it, plant the seed that the DBA won't be around forever. Wouldn't it be nice to have someone on staff who already knew the basics of how the company's databases work? That idea might encourage them to start an internal mentoring program.

Luck, Preparation, and Opportunity

If there is one thing I have learned through my days playing and coaching sports, it is that luck can be defined as when preparation meets opportunity. With that in mind I started attending those junior DBA classes. I was a sponge, soaking up everything possible. Over time I would ask to perform some routine tasks and was able to get some quality on-the-job training. It got to the point that when the regular DBAs (both of them) needed to take a day off, they could do so and send people my way for any issues.

I became more and more comfortable handling a lot of routine operational tasks. Backups, restores, password resets, creation of logins, and even some performance tuning and troubleshooting. I also started getting involved in configuring the necessary monitoring for the environment, helping to build an in-house monitoring solution to help us stay proactive for resolving issues. And I still had my regular day job working with PowerBuilder, .NET, and SQR reports.

And then, one day, all of my preparation met the opportunity it was waiting for. The regular DBAs resigned at the end of the calendar year. One was a contractor that left for a new contract somewhere else. The other simply did not want to stay any longer. Their manager came over to talk with my manager and then they asked me if I wanted to be the next DBA. One of my team members remarked about how the job was "a huge opportunity for you," and I went into the office to talk with the two managers about the position.

I told them I needed some time to think it over. Hey, I didn't want to seem too eager!

SOMETIMES YOU MAKE YOUR OWN LUCK

by Jonathan Gennick

"Sometimes you make your own luck." A friend once said those words to me after I'd landed a position that turned out to be pivotal to my career. I had worked a contract job in COBOL for two or three months to put bread on the table. Then the client abruptly pulled the plug on the project, sending a dozen or more of us out into the job market again.

My love at the time was SQL, so I had taken every opportunity to be involved with the database end of the project. I had wound up "owning" the input/output routines, because I knew both COBOL and Rdb, and I knew how to put them together. I worked carefully, had a good attitude, and exhibited passion for what I was doing. Looking back, I did excellent work, and I shared my excitement about that work with my coworkers.

One of my office mates—we were three to an office on that project—paid me more notice than I had realized. He later sought me out and was instrumental in bringing me on board with an international consulting firm. It was there that I learned Oracle, which led to my writing some books, which led to a career change (again due to passion and preparation), which led to my being able to live in the Upper Peninsula, where I'd long dreamed of living. I've been "lucky" several times in my career. In all cases that come to mind, though, what Tom says is true. Any "luck" has always been the result of work and preparation, and personal growth meeting the unexpected opportunity.

Community

All those events feel like they were a lifetime ago. Actually two lifetimes ago, since I have had two children since all of the above happened. Along the way, I knew I could not possibly know everything there is to know about being a DBA, so I reached out to find other DBAs. I found them on web sites, in forums, and at conferences. It's at the point now where I tell people the line, "You don't just get me, you get my network."

Before too much time had passed, I found myself doing some writing, helping others, and presenting sessions as well. In 2009 I was appointed to the PASS Board of Directors and I also became a SQL MVP. Not too bad for a PowerBuilder developer.

So that's how I ended up becoming a DBA. Many people, me included, are always curious to know how someone becomes a DBA. In a lot of cases, we end up here by accident, but there are also times when we simply prepare for our opportunity. My story is not necessarily unique, and certainly not the only one out there. I asked some colleagues if they would be willing to share their stories as well, and their replies follow.

Other Journeys

There are a lot of different paths toward becoming a DBA. I am far from the only person to have taken a roundabout way. Most of us do tend to have some technical experience or acumen, and have good organizational or analytical skills. But the truth is that those very same skills apply to a lot of other professions as well. For example, a hotel manager would need to be organized, pay attention to details, and be able to understand and troubleshoot the point-of-sale software that runs the registers.

There are few if any colleges or universities that offer database administration as a major. Lots of schools will offer computer science, or some type of information systems major, but nothing dedicated to being a DBA. Maybe a course or two on database design or theory, but probably not much on disaster recovery, high availability, server configurations, and everything else a DBA needs to know. So it is understandable that the path to becoming a DBA is not a straight line for most. In fact, we all tend to fall into the role at some point, and once there we decide whether we enjoy the work or not.

TIP: Buck Woody teaches a DBA course at the University of Washington. Enroll if you can.

Pharmacist

After 16 years of being a pharmacist where she helped to configure some Microsoft Access applications, Kathi decided to leave the hospital she was working at and get a job as a programmer. She learned some Visual Basic 4 and HTML, created her first ASP web site, and started working with SQL Server 6.5. After being placed for a six-month programming assignment, she was then hired by that same company as a full-time DBA. She is now a published author and a SQL Server MVP.

Hotel Manager

While working the most awful hours imaginable as a hotel manager, as well as dealing with some of the surliest customers possible, Brent stumbled upon Quattro Pro and spreadsheets. Tired of working the long hours, especially on holidays, he decided to switch over and get a job in IT. The hours got slightly better, except now he had to wear a pager all day and night, so it was actually a step backward. But he got to learn a lot about servers and eventually databases. Today he is also a SQL Server MVP.

Estimating Supervisor

I had no idea that such a job title even existed, but this is exactly where Tim started many years ago. The job was less than satisfying, and a friend got him started on some self-learning for T-SQL. He jumped at the chance to job-hop even though it meant he was to become an Access developer. That same company that hired him to be a developer decided to switch him to become their SQL Server DBA, an opportunity that he did not want at the time. But ten years later, he feels very fortunate to have been given the chance to be the DBA, and he is also a SQL Server MVP.

MUMPS Programmer

Jonathan was a MUMPS programmer at a major chemical company, supporting industrial hygiene and medical systems written in MUMPS and running under DEC VAX/VMS. One day he was told that the decision had been made to rewrite the systems using a relational database for the back-end storage.

The company was planning to standardize on Rdb, so Jonathan typed "HELP RDB" into his VMS command line. He devoured the online help. He devoured the manuals. He created databases to experiment with. He became enamored of the power of SQL, and quickly became the go-to person in is department for database questions. He wanted to become a DBA.

He failed to become a DBA as a MUMPS programmer. He got laid off instead.

He failed to become a DBA as a COBOL programmer at various contract jobs.

He failed to become a DBA as a Visual Basic programmer.

He almost failed to become a DBA as a PowerBuilder programmer.

Then one day the DBA quit, and Jonathan became Johnny-on-the-spot. He could finally call himself a DBA.

What made the difference for Jonathan is that he kept at it—for more than five years. He did quality work in all the development languages that he had to work in to put bread on the table, but he kept plugging away at his database skills.

When the DBA quit, that's when preparation met opportunity.

YOU'RE DRAFTED!

by Ken Simmons

It seems like most of the stories here are about people actively trying to become a DBA. I kept waiting for the scenario where the manager comes in and says to the developer, "Hey you, you're the DBA now."

Your Journey

If you are looking to become a DBA, how and where do you get started? Do you get a specific degree? Do you try to land a junior DBA job somewhere? How do you get your DBA career started without having experience as a DBA? What options do you have for breaking into this career path?

As with most professional fields, becoming a DBA can seem daunting. It can be tough to get started as a DBA because most of the time it comes down to someone giving you the break that you need. You need someone to give you the right opportunity, and before you can get that opportunity, you need to start preparing yourself. And how, exactly, are you to prepare yourself for a job you do not know much about?

LIFE EXPERIENCE—GET SOME

by Brent Ozar

Even schooling doesn't guarantee a DBA job. A company's most precious, valuable, and irreplaceable asset is its data. Companies have to know that their DBA is trustworthy and experienced, which means they don't usually trust people fresh out of college in the DBA role. As you review this chapter and the stories of how people became DBAs, think about how your own life experience can convey your trustworthiness.

Get Prepared

If you have decided that you want to become a DBA, then start taking steps to be ready for when opportunity comes knocking. If you take no action and sit around waiting for someone to hand you an opportunity for your dream job, then do not get upset when your break never comes. It won't.

What steps can you take to get yourself prepared? My first suggestion is to find opportunities in your everyday job that allow for you to gain some DBA experience. If you are not already in the IT industry, then your options will be more limited, but not impossible. If you are in IT, perhaps as a developer, then start getting more involved in database design work or performance tuning.

If you are a developer and are looking to become a DBA, I will give you a rather large tip on how to gain valuable experience: learn to get better at performance tuning without crying that you need to be "sa" in order to do the job. Seriously, if you know the system so well that you can get details about performance without being given administrative rights, then you are more than halfway to becoming a DBA.

You would be quite surprised to find out that many DBAs perform frequent job tasks without needing sa rights. And as more and more companies get tighter controls around the levels of access allowable, you may find it necessary to learn to get things done with the least amount of privileges.

> **TIP:** Learn to perform tasks without being a member of the sys admin fixed-server role. Such skills will serve you well later on.

If your current role does not allow for you to take on additional tasks that may be DBA-related, then go find one of the DBAs at work and ask them how you can get started. Most DBAs are always willing to help someone else learn more about the system; doing so means less support work when they are called upon to fix your mistakes! Most DBAs are both driven *and* lazy; this means that we are always looking for ways to make our lives easier. One way is to help train people on how to do their jobs better.

What if there is nothing for you to help with at work? You can look to volunteer your time. Many charitable organizations need people to donate their time. It is possible that a local church could use some help with their computers, perhaps even to help maintain a database or two. It may not be a 10TB database with 15,000 transactions per second, but it is a database, and it will be a learning opportunity for you to use on your resume.

BE A GOOD STEWARD

by Ken Simmons

It may be worth noting that data is still data, and that even though you are a volunteer, you need to be careful not to bite off more than you can chew and make a serious mistake. A programming mistake is not as disastrous as a DBA mistake. Be as responsible in your volunteer work as in your paid work.

If you are not interested in volunteering your time to help others, then perhaps you have an overlapping hobby that allows for a learning opportunity. In my case, I love Fantasy Football. Years ago I helped build a custom web site with a database back end. This gave me lots of learning opportunities that helped me when I got my initial opportunity to become a DBA.

Still another way for you to get prepared is to look online for part-time help. You may find someone that is willing to offer some contract work to help out with a database during nights and weekends. Such positions do exist, even for people with little to no experience. In most cases, they can directly lead to junior DBA roles. I would caution you to stay away from job advertisements that seem too good to be true; they usually are.

Get Trained

Part of your overall preparation should include some form of training. This training can come in various forms such as training books, classroom training, and online training; or, in the cases just mentioned, on-the-job training. Other sources of training would include seminars or conferences.

No matter what training medium you choose, it is vital that you get started. Even current DBAs have an ongoing training regime in place, so it is to your benefit to start getting into a similar habit. Start reading some web sites on a daily basis. Look for some recommended books. Set aside time in each day that you use strictly for training purposes. And if you are looking for the most valuable training method in order to expedite your own learning curve, then I have one word for you: teach.

If you truly want to learn a topic or subject, then try to teach it to someone else. Take some aspect of database administration, perhaps indexes, and try to explain how they work to someone else. You will find that the more you are asked to teach, the more in-depth knowledge you will acquire, and the better you will become.

I have often been asked by people about what type of degree they should consider getting if they want to become a DBA. I will simply say that your degree does not matter as much as you might think. In general, your degree is simply a measure of work, nothing more. And all the education in the world matters very little unless you also have motivation. When you combine an education with motivation, then you truly have a powerful force.

Get Certified

A lot has been written about the value of certifications. I believe that certifications have a place in communicating your overall value for others to see. I do *not* believe that certifications tell the complete story about who you are or your abilities.

If you believe that focusing on obtaining certifications is going to be your key to landing a DBA job quickly, you may be surprised to find out that many people will not hire you based solely on your certifications. If you are able to combine certifications with some level of relevant work experience, then you are going to find more doors opened than just having certifications without any relevant work experience.

The trouble with certifications is that many companies offer "boot camps" where you can spend one or two weeks and walk away certified in a particular piece of technology. The reason this is a problem is that it cheapens the certifications earned by others. This makes it difficult for potential employers to know if your certification represents your actual knowledge or if it represents your knowledge after two weeks of dedicated training that you have mostly forgotten by now.

> **TIP:** Certification and experience are a powerful combination, similar to when you combine an education with motivation.

Also keep in mind that there are many people out there that are good enough to be certified but never bother to take the exams. In fact, most people only take the exams as a stepping stone to something else. If a person believes they have nowhere else to step, why would they bother taking the exam? In other words, *not* being certified does not necessarily hurt you, providing you have some experience to back up your credentials. But for people that don't have requisite experience, they may look to get certified. Potential employers weigh this when they meet with candidates.

My advice would be to gain some experience first and get certified second. Doing it the other way around may raise a red flag. And you would not want to invest a lot of time and money into something that will not pay off until after you find the job you were hoping the certification itself would help you find, right? You might as well invest your time in finding ways to get real-world experience first.

Now Go and Get Your Opportunity!

You've gotten prepared, you have some experience, and you have some training and possibly even a certification. Now is the time to go and find yourself a job as a DBA, right?

Well, not exactly. See, the time to get started on finding a DBA job is not after you have all these things, it is *before* you have them. Do not wait until you think you have all the necessary skills; you may never be comfortable enough with your skills to think that anyone would want to hire you as a DBA. Instead, start looking for work right away.

Most jobs are found through networking with friends and family. Start letting people know you are looking for a job as a DBA as soon as you know that you want to have such a job. Why? Because a proper job search can take months. In between the time you get a proper job search started and the time you finally get your opportunity, you will be able to get the experience and training necessary to hit the ground running.

Start talking with people. Tell then what you are looking for. Tell them what you want to do. You may find that those opportunities already exist right where you are. And if not, then at least you are planting seeds in the back of people's minds. The idea is that they may come across an opportunity that you might be interested in, and you want them to think of you when they do. And the only way for them to know you are interested is to tell them.

Be proactive. Take ownership of your career. Take charge of your future. Be prepared for your opportunity and let someone else remark, "Hey, how did they get so lucky to become a DBA?"

Staying Focused

Chances are that it can take you quite some time to get your opportunity to become a DBA. In my case, it took about five years from the time I first told my managers that I wanted to become a DBA until the time I finally got my chance at a different company. During that time there were lots of chances for me to simply give up. But I *knew* that I wanted to become a DBA, so I stayed after it and finally got my big break.

For me, the key was to periodically visualize the job that I wanted. The more I started to think about the job I wanted, the more I found myself doing a handful of those tasks during my day. Even to this day I am always visualizing what I want my dream job to be like. And every now and then I take two big steps back, look upon my workday, and realize that I am already doing a lot of the things that keep me energized.

I am often reminded of a quote from Vince Lombardi: "Once you learn to quit, it becomes a habit." If you want to change jobs and transition into a new role, whether it is at your company or somewhere new, then you need to not be easily discouraged. It will take time for everything to fall into place. You simply must believe in yourself. After all, if you don't believe in yourself, why should anyone else?

Keep learning, keep writing, keep speaking, keep meeting new people, and keep your eye on the prize. Continue to prepare yourself for your opportunity so that you can smile when someone asks you, "Hey, how did you get so lucky to be a DBA?"

Chapter 2

Now What Do I Do?

Now that your dream has come true and you are the resident database administrator, what do you do first? Like any other job in the world you need to get started on...well... something, right? But what? Where do you focus your energies in order to best demonstrate your value to your organization? Knowing where to begin is crucial for your success, and this chapter is going to help you best determine how to get started, plan for your first one hundred days, and even decide who you should eat lunch with on a regular basis.

> **TIP:** You are going to be constantly judged by your tangible results from this point forward.

In this chapter, we will discuss the following:

1. Putting together your initial checklist

2. What to do with the information you have gathered

3. Responding to unfamiliar alerts

4. How to break the ice

5. Mr. Right

What You Have in Common with the President

Do you really have anything in common with the President? Yes. More than you probably realize. First, about half of the people around you doubt whether you are qualified to actually hold the job you have been given. Second, every time you make a decision or plot a course of action, you will constantly be criticized, even by your supporters. And third, you are going to be judged by what you accomplish in your first one hundred days, good or bad, even if it is not in your control.

Every four years we elect a new President, and the person in office is always subject to approval ratings. You will have your own version of this fact of life; it is called your annual performance review. Come review time, you want your approval ratings to be as high as possible.

Sound awful? Perhaps, but it really is not all that bad as long as you are aware of these things when you start. The most important objective for you is your plan of action for when you first arrive. If you think you can show up, grab a cup of coffee, and ease into your new position, then you are mistaken. Your cup of coffee can wait until after you start gathering the information you need in order to do your new job effectively.

And what information is that? How about some of the basics first, such as, what servers are you responsible for? What applications are you expected to support? What time of day are the applications used? Who are your customers? Are the databases being backed up properly right now? How would you know if the backups were failing? With so many items to check, it can become very overwhelming very fast. That is why you need to put together a checklist of the bare essentials and get started. Then, after you are able to get a handle on your environment, you can start making some short-term plans for improvements. Before you know it, your first one hundred days will be behind you and you will be able to look back and see just how far you have come in a short amount of time.

Trust me, it is easier than it sounds, you just need to be organized.

Your Initial Checklist

By now you should be sitting at your desk on what we will call day one. Your initial meetings with HR are over, you have gotten a tour of the place, and you are making certain you have the access you need to at least get started. Things like e-mail, for example. Oh, and access to the database servers they expect you to administer.

That is the very first piece of information you need, right? *What servers and systems am I responsible for?* Without that little nugget of knowledge, it is going to be very difficult to make any headway as you start your long, slow journey upstream.

Your initial checklist is divided into sections. Why? Well, because I like to put things into lists and categorize the lists if possible. It just helps me remember the bigger picture and not worry about missing any particular detail. I would encourage you to try the same thing and see if it helps, but everyone organizes themselves in different ways, so don't worry if you want to start your list differently.

Now, the checklist has three main sections. One section pertains to gathering information on what I simply call *your stuff*. Another section deals with finding information on *the customer's stuff*. Still another section you need to consider is what I call *your action plans*. Those three areas are where you will start to focus your efforts on day one; find your stuff, find your customer's stuff, and start making an action plan. So, a sample of a checklist might look like this:

1. Create a list of servers.

2. Check that database backups are running.

3. Spot check and verify that you can do a restore from one of those backups.

4. Build a list of customers.

5. List the "most important" databases.

6. List upcoming deliverables/projects.

7. Establish environmental baselines.

    a. Server configuration check

    b. Database configuration check

8. Compose your recovery plan (not your backup plan, your recovery plan).

Notice that my checklist is missing a few things that a lot of people will tell you are a must for DBAs to be doing daily. It doesn't include things like routine index maintenance, performance tuning, reviewing event logs, and so on. Sure, all of those things are necessary, but we are still on your list of items for day one. Everything I have mentioned so far is going to take you more than a few days to gather. If you get tied up troubleshooting some stored procedure on day one, then you are setting yourself up for a massive failure should a disaster hit and you have not had time to document your recovery plan.

Would you rather be a hero for telling that developer to stop writing cursors or a hero for informing a customer that you can have their database back up and running in less than 30 minutes? I know which choice I would make so soon after taking a new position.

> **TIP:** These tasks will all take longer than a day to perform, but do not delay in getting the checklist started.

On your first day, explain to your manager that you'll be gathering this inventory data first. By taking the initiative to perform due diligence first, you're showing them that your first mission is to safeguard their data, your job, and their job too. They probably won't be able to produce the inventory for you, and they're going to want it even more than you do. You will have plenty of time later on for the other stuff, and it will fall naturally into your environment baseline and subsequent action plans as you bring standards to your enterprise.

AN OSHA MOMENT

by Brent Ozar

At one company, when I laid out this plan for my first two weeks, my boss said out loud: "Holy sh*t! We don't have this information for the rest of our servers either." He then pulled his sys admins in, told them to drop what they were doing, and to do the same thing I was doing—but for the file servers, Exchange servers, etc.

Let's look at why each of the items in the checklist is important, and important to address from day one. If today is your first day, you want to begin these tasks right now.

Create a List of Servers

Not sure I really need to explain this one, but you best get an idea of exactly what you are expected to administer. Chances are your initial list will not be complete, but it will give you an immediate baseline of reference. Trust me, at some point some person will walk up to you and start talking about a server you never knew existed. And they will be very confused as to why you have never heard of it, since they work with it all the time, there is a database there, and you are the DBA.

Do your best to gather as much information right away as you can. That way you will know more about what you are up against, and it will help you when it comes time to formulate your action plans, which will be very different depending on whether you have five or five hundred instances to look after.

I know what you are asking yourself. You are asking, "Self, how do I find out what I am responsible for?" I suggest you start with your immediate supervisor and go from there. The trail may take you to application managers and server administrators. For example, your boss might say that you are responsible for the payroll databases. But what are "the payroll databases"? You may need to run with that initial bit of information and do some detective work to track down the specific databases involved. Along your journey, you will be given an overview of the complexity that is your new home. Any detective work that you're forced to do will pay off handsomely by deepening you knowledge and understanding of where you work.

If you are looking for a technical solution to finding databases, there are a handful of ways to get the job done. One of the simplest ways is to use the SQLCMD utility with the –L parameter to return a list of database servers that are broadcasting on the network. Since it is possible that some servers may not be found with that tool, you would be wise to still ask around when putting together your list.

And where do you keep such a list? I like to keep a lot of notes written down in a notebook. When I say "notebook," I'm not talking about a computer. I'm talking about a physical, paper book that I can hold in my hands. Others prefer to put everything into Word documents and store them on their computer. The paper notebook works best for me because I have found that I learn better by rote than by typing. What I write with a pen stays with me better than what I type with a keyboard.

One more thing to mention would be the importance of having a list of servers you are *not* responsible for. There is a chance that you have some systems in your environment that are maintained strictly by vendors. If something goes wrong with one of those servers, it is important to know who is responsible for what. And if someone tells you that you do not need to worry about a server, my advice would be to get that in writing. Believe me, when disaster strikes, you had better be able to provide proof about the systems that are your responsibility.

If you are storing your information in a spreadsheet or similar document, then you can go back over time to better track how your environment is changing. Are you administering more servers or fewer? More databases or fewer? Are all your jobs running? Backups working? This information will surely help with your approval ratings. If nothing else, you'll have the backup detail to be able to clearly show to your boss how your job is changing and how your responsibilities are increasing. You'll be better able to document your value to the company.

ON SELLING YOUR VALUE

by Jonathan Gennick

You'd think your boss would know your value, would know what it is that you do all day long. My own experience though, is quite opposite that. Early in my career I suffered a painful layoff. Looking back on that event, I've come to believe it was in part because I failed to manage upwards in a way that kept my boss apprised of my true value to the company. My boss was local, in the same building. My internal clients were all over the country, with some even in Europe. I worked closely with those internal clients, delivering results. But my boss was outside the loop. He and I didn't interact much. We never really needed to interact on a daily basis, so we didn't. Guess who got the boot when the mandate came down to cut head count?

I learned many painful lessons from that first layoff. One is that bosses are busy people. Your boss has his own set of responsibilities. He may have only a dim idea as to what exactly you do. Make sure that you do a better job than I did at keeping your boss "in the loop" and apprised of your good work. Someday your boss will be in a meeting with HR about cutting staff. When he's in that meeting, you want him to be able to recall from the top of his head all the good that you do for the company.

Check Database Backups

Now that you know what servers you are responsible for, your next question had better be, are the backups running?" Do not assume that everything is working perfectly. Dig into the details yourself and verify that each and every instance is being backed up. Oh, and that includes the system databases (master, model, msdb) as well as all user databases. Check that the backup files exist, that the directory they are being stored in is on a disk that has adequate space, and if there have been any recent failures.

You will also want to note the backup schedule for the servers and databases. You can use that information later on to verify that the databases are being backed up to meet the business requirements. You would not want to find out that the business is expecting a point-in-time restore ability for a database that is only being backed up once a week.

I cannot stress this enough, but if there is one and only one thing for you to focus on as a DBA, it is to ensure that you can recover in the event of a disaster. And any good recovery plan starts with having a reliable database backup strategy.

Verify That You Can Restore

Every now and then I like to do a spot check of my backups by taking some and attempting to restore. For me, I like to attempt a same-server restore as well as a restore to a different instance. Note that this is not the same as just restoring the file header in order to verify that the file is readable. No sir, I want to restore the entire database—it's just my preference. I would not typically have time to verify each and every backup file, and would not attempt to do so. I just want to select a few backup files from a few servers and ensure that there are no issues.

Now, I said a "same-server restore" in the last paragraph and I want to make something very clear:

> *Be mindful when performing a same-server restore to a* production server.

There, now I feel better. Same-server restores should be done only when you know it is safe to do so. How do you know if it is safe? Well, you could always ask someone. Or you could look to see if people are currently connected to the instance. Or, if your database is fairly small and manageable, and the restore should only take a few minutes at most, it should be safe. And of course, if it is a non-production server, then you can feel safer.

Which databases should you verify can be restored? You could focus your efforts on just about any group or set of databases. The real goal here is for you to become familiar with the restore process in your new shop as well as to verify that the backups are usable. Make certain you know all aspects of the recovery process for your shop before you start poking around on any system of importance. It could save you some embarrassment later on should you sound the alarm that a backup is not valid and what turns out to not be valid is really just your understanding of how things work.

> **TIP:** Another good reason to practice restores is so that you can perform one when the call comes in at 3:00 a.m. the morning after you've stayed up late three nights in a row. You'll be tired. You won't be thinking clearly. The practice that you've previously put in will serve as your brain's "muscle memory." Practice makes you better able to do the right thing under pressure and when fatigued.

Build a List of Customers

If you know what servers you are responsible for, then start asking who the customers are for each of those servers. Note that this line of inquiry can result in a very large list. And with shared systems, you could find that everyone has a piece of every server.

The list of customers is vital information to have. For example, if there is a need to reboot a server, it is nice to know who you need to contact in order to explain that the server will be offline for five minutes while it is rebooted. And while you compile your list of customers, it does not hurt to know who the executives are and which servers they are most dependent upon.

When you start listing the customers, you should also start asking about the applications and systems those customers use, and the time of day they are being used the most. You may be surprised to find some systems that people consider to be relatively minor are used throughout the day, while other systems that are considered most important are used only once a month.

There is an extra benefit to building this list: you get your chance to begin building a relationship with your customers. Chances are they will be flattered that you care enough to seek them out. Putting together your list gives you an excuse to reach out to your customers. Think of it as an ice breaker—an easy excuse for the two of you to meet.

INFREQUENTLY USED DATABASES CAN STILL BE CRITICAL

by Ken Simmons

Tom's time-of-day comment made me think back to when I used to work managing a data warehouse. We had a database that could be offline three weeks out of the month, and nobody would notice. It was a critical database, with a specific purpose. The workload just happened to be such that the database wasn't used three weeks out of the month. It sure was used during week 1 though. During week 1, it had better be up 24/7. The remaining weeks, it didn't matter so much. The moral? Don't assume a correlation between how much something is used and how truly important it is.

List the "Most Important" Databases

While you gather your list of you important customers, go one step further and find out what their most important databases are. This could be done by either (1) asking them or (2) asking others, and then (3) comparing those lists. You could be very surprised to find that they do not match. You will be even more surprised to find how many people can forget about some of their systems and need a gentle reminder about their importance. As DBAs, we treat all databases with equal importance, but we recognize that some databases are indeed more important than others, especially given a particular time of day, week, or month.

For example, you could have a mission-critical data warehouse. Everyone in the company could tell you that this system is vital. What they cannot tell you, however, is that it is only used for three days out of the month. So, the database could be offline for 21 days and no one would say a word.

Another example would be a trading platform. This system could be used heavily for nine or ten hours each business day. But for the remaining hours of the day it is not used at all. Does that mean that when these systems are not used they are not important? No, it does not. What it does mean is that you are gathering more details about the systems. If 17 different groups mention some tiny database, but they consider it to be of minor importance, you can consider it very important because it is touched by so many different people.

Another factor here is recoverability. If the business requires you to be able to recover a database to a point in time, then you should consider that to be an important database as well, even if that customer sits across from you and says "it's not *that* important." I have lost track of the number of times a customer has told me offhand that "the system really is not a big deal—we need to recover to within five minutes, and we use it all day long, but you don't have to worry about it." Yeah, right. Until a disaster happens, of course, and you are on the hook to put everything back, and quickly!

List Upcoming Projects and Deliverables

If there is someone around that can help you see the current and upcoming projects, it would help for you to know what is about to be dumped in your lap. You want to minimize the number of surprises that await you; knowing what projects are currently planned helps you to understand how much time you will be asked to allocate for each one. And do keep in mind that you will be expected to maintain a level of production support in addition to your project support, in addition to the action tasks you are about to start compiling.

You'll also want to know which servers will be decommissioned in the near future so that you don't waste time performance tuning servers that are on death row. Keep an eye on this angle as well.

Establish Environmental Baselines

Baselining your environment is a function that gets overlooked frequently. The importance of having a documented starting point cannot be stressed enough. Without a starting point as a reference, it will be difficult for you to chart and report upon your progress over time.

The idea of gathering baseline information on the servers you administer is to simply find out how many deviations you have from an ideal state. You have already done one baseline item—you have evaluated your database backups. Since this checklist item can become a little cumbersome in a short amount of time, try to focus on the basics.

For example, on a stand-alone database server with direct attached storage, your data files should exist on a separate drive from your log files. How many servers have that same configuration? And what about those disk drives? Is there a standard RAID configuration? (You may be surprised to find that servers are not always physically built the same.) How about the memory settings or the number of processors for the instances? How big are the data and log files, and what is the average CPU utilization?

Focus on a handful of big-ticket items to gather as your baseline information and keep the information going forward. You can add additional items over time as needed.

I would also advise you to streamline the ways in which you collect this information. For example, if you have one hundred servers, you really do not want to remote to all of them just to examine the memory settings for each one. You will need to learn how to efficiently gather your information, much of which can be collected using tools such as System Center Configuration Manager (SCCM) and Operations Manager. If your environment does not have those tools, then you may need to script out your baseline queries using PowerShell, T-SQL, or some alternative.

Alternatively, you could use a defined central management server in SQL 2008 to run queries against multiple instances at the same time. Or you could look to use policy-based management to report on and possibly enforce configuration options. No matter what method you choose, the goal remains the same: to track changes over time. Once you've captured a picture of how your environment looks now, you can start to document how to return servers to their original state if something goes wrong.

Compose Your Recovery Plan

Notice how I said "recovery plan" as opposed to "backup plan." In your checklist so far, you have already verified that your database backups are running, started to spot check that you can restore from your backups, and gotten an idea of your important databases. Now is the time to put all of this together in the form of a disaster recovery (DR) plan. For each one of those databases listed as important, you should write down exactly the steps involved to recover should a disaster happen.

Make no mistake about it: should a disaster happen, then your job is on the line. If you fail to recover because you are not prepared, then you could easily find yourself reassigned to "special projects" by the end of next week. The best way to avoid that happening to you is to practice, practice, practice. Your business should have some scheduled DR tests perhaps once a year, but that should not prevent you from doing your own smaller DR tests on a more frequent basis.

Document each system and all the steps required to recover. Is the database in full-recovery mode? How frequently are you doing transaction log backups? Write down the backup schedule so that it is clear where the restore points are. If your customers expect recovery to the minute and you are in simple mode, then you are heading for a true disaster.

And don't forget about recovering from past days or weeks. If your customer needs a database backup restored from two months ago, make certain you know every step in the process in order to get that job done. If your company uses an offsite tape storage company, and if it takes two days to recall a tape from offsite, then you need to communicate that fact to your users ahead of time as part of your DR plans.

You Have Your Info, Now What?

Everything discussed up to this point should keep you busy until at least lunchtime on day one. OK, maybe it will take you a few days to get all of the information on your checklist. You may or may not have a lot of that information already available, so the amount of time it takes to gather everything will depend upon the current structure of your particular department in your shop. (By the way, get used to hearing and saying "it depends"; more on that later.) No worries, because you can transition into the next phase while you continue to gather your data.

Meet with Your Manager

While gathering the data, you should meet with your manager to discuss your preliminary findings and work together to prioritize the work that needs to be done. If you have found one server that is not running any backups, or the backups are failing, then that server must take precedence over everything else. I don't care which one of your "most important" customers screams at you on day one to fix a query they wrote that filled up a 70GB log drive, you *must* ensure you can recover from a disaster.

Continue to review your checklist with your manager and determine which items need to be done, which items need the most resources and effort, and which ones can wait for now. It is very important that you and your new manager agree upon the tasks and their priority before you get started. This will serve both of you very well; it gives you a chance to be measured from this point forward.

Should you and your manager disagree, however, with regard to your priorities, make sure you have that documented. It will serve you well when someone comes around asking why something specific has not been done yet, and you politely explain why you have been working on something else. Then, if there is still disagreement, you, the other person, and your boss can get together to reevaluate your priorities.

> **TIP:** Document, but not to be confrontational. Don't whack your boss upside the head with his old e-mails. Instead, use them as gentle reminders that you are committed to working on the priorities that your boss lays down. Your boss will appreciate that you are putting your efforts toward his priorities.

After you have met with your manager, you are going to constantly be measured. Everyone is going to want or need you for one thing or another. Every interaction you have with others will serve as a form of measurement, to be verified by something tangible produced by actions on your part. If you have that checklist, and your manager is aware of the checklist, you now have something tangible to deliver on starting from day one.

Think about how important this will be for you. In three or four weeks someone, somewhere, will ask your manager how things are working out with the new DBA. Your manager will be able to quickly affirm all the great work you have been doing (let's just assume you have been doing great work and not sitting on your arse all day). You will be able to track your progress easily, and eventually you can prepare a brief summary or presentation that details your progress over your first few months.

Meet with the Developers

If your company has in-house development teams, take some time to meet and greet them. They are going to figure most prominently in your success in the coming months. Find out what projects they are working on and what roadblocks they are currently facing, and see if there is an opportunity for you to offer assistance.

There is no question that the developers are going to keep you very busy. The developers will be the ones that look to push the limits with the technologies at their disposal. The end result will be an abundance of little training opportunities for you to take advantage of. Fill up the transaction log? Let me understand more about what you were trying to do. Filled up the entire log drive? Your remote query has bad performance? Your stored procedure with 27 nested cursors is taking too long? Here, let me help you with that, and perhaps we can find a better way to get the job done.

Will every developer want to be your friend? Absolutely not—it is rare to be somewhere where everyone gets along at all times. If you come across a developer that believes they know more than anyone else in the room, you can sit back and chuckle because you already know that the DBAs are the smartest, otherwise you wouldn't always be called to fix their problems all day long.

Meet with the Server Administrators

Depending on your shop, you may or may not have duties. Many DBAs focus only on the administration of the server instances and leave the O/S administration to others. If that is the case for you, then you need to make an effort to get to know this team. The server administrators have their fingers on the pulse of the whole company. They know which systems are most important, and they know where to find some extra hardware when you are in a pinch.

SYS ADMINS ARE YOUR FRIENDS

by Jonathan Gennick

It's a huge help if you are on friendly terms with the sys admins that manage your servers. If a DBA can be comfortable in sitting down with a sys admin to troubleshoot a problem together, well, I'm not sure it gets any better than that.

System administrators are also going to be the ones to build out your infrastructure. It is vital that you are aware of the hardware you are using, as well as the hardware that might be coming in the door. If your company is looking to implement a storage area network (SAN), they will not be asking you how to configure it; they will be asking someone on the server team. Since a SAN can and will have dramatic impacts on database servers, you need to be involved in those discussions. Ideally you will be invited to the table to discuss such things early on, and the more time you spend with the server team, the better chance you have to know about what changes are coming your way.

You are also going to frequently be needed to help the developers and the server administrators talk to and understand each other. Why is that the case? Well, think of yourself as the universal translator. Developers know code, and they know various facets of the business; and because they focus on those items daily, they are not spending time racking servers, installing routers, replacing hard disks, allocating space on the SAN, and so forth. Server administrators do those things, but they do not know how to code or build applications that will drive the business forward at the same speed as a developer.

Unfortunately these two groups rarely interface unless there is a problem (or an opportunity to point fingers at each other). That is where you come in. The developers can point their fingers at you and explain what the roadblock is at the moment, and you can turn and speak to the server administrators in a language they can understand. Without you, that does not happen, frustrations levels rise, and your shop ends up spending far too much money on hardware to solve issues that could be remedied by altering a few lines of code.

So by meeting with both groups, you continue to brush up on your language skills and help to keep the peace, and ultimately you can also help to reduce costs.

Meet with Your Customers

By now you have met with almost everyone possible, except for your actual customers. Actually, when you are a DBA, everyone is your customer, but let's focus on the actual end users of the applications and servers. These are the people that are going to give you a much different view than any other group.

Why is it so important to meet with them? Well, consider this story.

One day a man answered an ad for renting a bedroom above a garage at a family's home. The man was well kept and had a job (no one knew what it was), but was also always around. But he was a nice enough fellow and never late with his rent, and the family liked having him around. The family never noticed that the man always liked to go with them for rides in their car. It did not matter the destination; the man would ask, "Mind if I take a ride?" and the family would let him.

Every time he rode in the car he would ask one or two questions about the car, but not so many as to make the family think anything was strange. He would simply work the questions into a conversation somehow. "So, think they have enough cup holders in here?" could lead to all sorts of comments about the design and functionality of the car.

Eventually the man told the family it was time for him to move out; he had found a new apartment to live at. Before he left, he finally told them what he did for a living: he worked for the car company. The reason he asked those questions was to get honest feedback about the car's design. The feedback they provided was much more reliable and honest than any survey could hope to be; the man observed the family actually using the product!

And so you need to do the same with your end users. Get to understand more about how they are using their tools, what their frustrations are, and what little things would help them (and therefore your business) be more efficient and productive. Go and ask your customers if you can take a ride in their car. You will be amazed at the things you will find.

Is That Alert Serious?

So, you have collected your info. You have meet with all sorts of people. And you get back to your desk to find about 1,500 e-mails waiting for you. What to do? Some of those e-mails might be database alerts. Better look into those.

> **TIP:** Setting up rules in your e-mail to file alerts automatically is a wonderful thing, but only when done carefully and correctly.

Is a specific alert important? I don't know. It could be. Or it might be safe to ignore. If it is really important, then someone will start yelling at you soon enough, right? Well, technically that may be true, but let's not let it come to that for you. Here is a basic rule to follow when it comes to alerts:

> *If you don't know what they are for, then you need to find out why you are getting them.*

Simple enough to remember. Following that rule will be the difference between you being thought of in a positive way vs. a negative way. Consider the following scenario: It's a lazy Sunday afternoon. You are relaxing at home. Your Blackberry receives a cryptic message that you don't understand. You assume that someone else must have gotten the same message and knows what to do about it, so you will be able to find out tomorrow what it means. The next morning at work, you have users complaining about one of the important databases. Reports and batch loads should have finished hours ago and are still running. The users want to know what the problem is and how long it will be before you fix things. You have no idea what the problem is, but you do remember that cryptic message from yesterday. You do some research, find out where the alert came from, find the message itself, start to understand what it might mean, and finally isolate the problem. You start to get the system back into working order, but by then it has essentially been out of the water for most of the day. No one else received the page—just you—and therefore all blame lies at your feet and your feet alone.

Sound like good times? It wasn't, and it describes an event that happened to me in my first few weeks on the job. Since that day I have made it my personal mission to make certain that any alerting system of mine would only provide value. Too many times I hear about shops where they are flooded with e-mails. Some are alerts, and some are just informational. I am always looking for things to be efficient, and that is why I only want alerts for items that are actionable.

So, let's assume that every alert that comes your way to start is something that requires action on your part. Note that I did not include this in the initial checklist, but only because responding to alerts should be secondary to the tasks discussed previously. How much sense would it be for you to spend hours respond to an alert for one of your least critical systems while the most critical system goes without a database backup for yet another day?

But now is the time to ask someone, "Hey! What is our alerting system?" If possible you should review the different types of alerts and see if they can be marked critical vs. an informational.

How can you judge the seriousness of the alert? How do you know if it is truly important? Simple—if it relates to one of the databases or customers that you are responsible for, then there is no question that you should look into the alert. If it is not one of the items listed previously, then there is no question that you should look into the alert. In other words, if you don't know the answer, then it must be yes.

> **TIP:** Remember, if you do not know how serious an alert is, then treat it as if it is very serious.

Should I Look Into That Alert?

Now that you that know any alert of unknown origin should be considered serious until proven otherwise, the real question becomes "what next"? If you have other people on your team, then your first stop would be to ask them. If it is just yourself, then ask your manager. If those two stops lead to dead ends, then you have a few other options at your disposal.

Review the Alert System

Start digging into the alert system to see if you can find out why the alert in question was generated. In doing so you will learn more about the alert system, making it easier to understand future alerts that may come your way. If the alert you worried about is for something straightforward like Database Mail sending you an e-mail based upon a failed job in SQL Server Agent, then your research effort should be easy. If the alert system is a little more complex, as in Operations Manager, then it may take a little longer to ascertain the details, but the extra effort now will be worth it in the long run.

And while reviewing the alert system, make certain it is not sending e-mails to one mailbox (yours) as opposed to a distribution list. Always use a distribution list to send your alert notifications, unless you plan on being available and responsive every minute of every day.

But what if you do not know how the e-mail was sent?

Ask the Developers

If you have already gathered details on the server or database involved in the alert, then go ask the developers if they have additional knowledge on the nature of the alert. They may be able to shed some light on events; perhaps a batch load failed or they were doing some testing. Worst case, it is a sign of something important, and they will be very glad that you have come to them before notifying anyone else.

But what if they have no additional details?

Ask the Server Administrators

The next logical step is to approach the server administrators. One of them might be familiar with the alert system or the nature of the alert itself. They may also have configured some e-mail rules that might be of benefit to you as well.

Ask around to see; again you may be uncovering something more serious than you realize, and the server team would be very glad to have you come to them before you were to contact…your customers.

Ask Your Customers

When all else fails, go ask the customers themselves to see if they are aware of any issues at the moment. You may find that they are having some troubles already, and they will be happy to see you. By helping them with any possible issues, you may also be able to uncover the nature of the alert. And if they are not having any issues at the moment, it will be beneficial if you raised awareness now so that they can contact you again later should any abnormalities arise.

Every time an alert comes in, you are being given the opportunity to learn something new. Embrace that and learn to love it, because if you do not it will quickly become the bane of your existence to the point that you want to throw your Crackberry against the wall.

And when that time comes, you will need to commiserate with someone, preferably over some food and beverages.

Hi, Want to Grab Some Lunch?

By this point you have done a basic health check on the systems, you know your customers, and you know which systems are most important, so it is time you start learning more about the people you will be working most closely with in the coming weeks and months.

> **TIP:** When starting a new job, everyone is a stranger. You need to learn how to meet others in order to develop mutually beneficial relationships.

Now, I am a very shy person by nature. Most people do not believe me when I tell them that, but it is very true. As such I have a hard time meeting new people, even people I work with. This makes it difficult for people to get to know me, and for me to know them. In turn that can make it difficult to have a strong, successful working relationship. If there is one thing I have learned over the years, it is the importance of managing relationships with those up and down the chain from you.

Meeting by Eating

How are people who are shy or naturally introverted able to build and manage relationships with others? It is not an easy thing to do. In fact, it can seem overwhelming at times. But I have found one very common trait that everyone shares: everyone eats.

It is true. At some point everyone will eat. You may find them sitting down to have lunch. You may find them going to get a cup of coffee in the morning. Chances are you are going to see everyone you work with, at one time or another, eating. And there is a good chance that you tend to eat from time to time as well. What's to stop you from eating together every now and then? To break the ice, go to someone else's office or cubicle around 11:45, introduce yourself as the new guy, and ask if they know of any good places to grab lunch in the area.

I take a walk to get a cup of coffee every morning. I do not always buy a cup for myself, but at least one person in the group does. So why do I go? Because the ten minutes I spend with them gives me ten more minutes of interaction with them outside of work that I would not have if I sit in my cubicle.

Every now and then I find myself having lunch, or walking to get lunch, with others. And on days when I feel like I have been eating too much, I head to the gym with a different group of coworkers. In other words, I have been able to find ways to interact with different groups of people in different ways in an effort for us to get to know each other a little better. Does that mean we always get along? Absolutely not. What it does mean is that we make an effort to get along.

Politicking, or Not

I must warn you against getting mired in office politics. That is a no-win situation for anyone. Aim for good, healthy relationships with coworkers. Healthy relationships are not about conspiring together and beating others down. Healthy relationships are about working together and building others up.

> **CAUTION:** Do not get mired into gossip or office politics.

Do not get involved in conjecture on others, gossip, or rumors. Stick to known facts only—not hearsay—and do not knowingly spread false information. Office politics can easily drag down morale, create divisions, and just make life miserable.

Dealing with Introversion

Not all technical people are introverted, but many are. The nature of our work calls for detail-oriented people comfortable at working alone for long periods of time. Those traits are in stark contrast to the outgoing salesperson who can meet 15 new people in 10 minutes, and be bosom-buddies with all of them. We are the people who can sit in a conference lecture with 100 other people and walk out not having met a single one of them.

Yet career success demands that we make ourselves visible. Sometimes we need to step up and lead, or present on what we know. We need to be comfortable in meeting people and working together. And we need to do all these things while being true to ourselves and respecting the personalities that we were born with.

Accept That Nothing Is Wrong

If you find that you're the sort of person to want to have lunch alone, do not despair. The very first thing that you should do is

Realize that you are not put together wrong.

Yes, it is true. If our entire society were made up of social bubbleheads running around and meeting each other, we'd all be in a world of hurt. We need those outgoing people. Your company needs its sales force, for example. But we need all the other personality types, too. Those salespeople need products and services to sell.

The key is to "know thyself." Know your own comfort zone. Play to your strengths. Develop skills that you lack. You can actually treat "extroversion" as just another skill to master. Doing so will pay handsomely in both personal and job satisfaction.

NOTE: A good book on personality traits is *Please Understand Me*, by David Keirsey and Marilyn Bates (Prometheus Nemesis, 1984).

Take Care of Yourself

The defining trait of an introvert is sometimes said to be that

An introvert draws energy from being alone, and expends energy to engage in social situations.

Does that sound like you? If it does, then don't be afraid to lay down some boundaries. For example, when travelling to conferences, my editor generally blocks out breakfast for himself. That's his "me time," when he can charge his batteries for the day. He also takes himself off the clock for lunch. He'll reach out aggressively to engage you if you walk by the Apress booth, but at lunch he switches off the "selling mode" and just enjoys a good meal.

When travelling with colleagues, don't feel obligated to spend every waking moment with them. There is nothing wrong with telling your coworkers that you need some time alone, and that you'd rather not go bar-hopping until 2:00 a.m. Be up front about why you're doing it. Your colleagues will understand. Some may admit to being in the same boat.

Did I just say to eat lunch with coworkers? I'm going to contradict myself now by giving you permission to eat alone if you need some space. Meals are a great venue in which to engage coworkers and get to know them better. But you don't have to spend each and every meal with them. Take care of yourself first. If you need lunch alone to get your head together for the afternoon, then take it.

Be Open and Straightforward

Don't try to be something you're not. Don't be afraid to admit that you're not a super-outgoing person. Sometimes when I want to meet someone, I just walk up and tell that person I'd like to meet them. It's a straightforward approach lacking in subtlety, but why not? If you take an interest in people, and attempt to befriend them, most people will respond positively regardless of how clumsy your own efforts are.

Join Some Organizations

Organizations provide structure. And that structure makes it easier to step outside of one's comfort zone. That's why organizations such as the Professional Association for SQL Server (PASS) are so valuable. They provide a socially safe venue in which to make professional contacts. That the other members are there for the same reason only helps.

Organizations also provide opportunities to lead, and to develop speaking and presentation skills. You can start small. You don't need to make your first talk in a 1,000-seat room. Start with a local user group. Work your way up as your comfort and confidence grow.

Don't make it all about work either. The skills and confidence that you develop working in a community or church organization easily translate into the professional space. If you can work with people to make a difference in your community, then you know you can do the same in your job.

Accept That Nothing Is Wrong

Did we just have this heading? We sure did, but the point is so important it bears repeating. It is a sad truth that society in general tends to smile upon bubbly and outgoing people, and to likewise frown upon those who are quiet and withdrawn. That's an unfortunate and wrongheaded attitude. Do not get sucked into it!

Everything I've said about developing people skills is intended with just that one goal in mind: to develop your people skills. Don't try to make yourself something you are not. Your personality is a big part of what makes you good at your job. Don't fight that goodness. Play to your strengths. At the same time, work to develop your skills in other areas. There is no contradiction in doing both of those things.

CONVERSATION STARTERS AND SMALL TALK

by Jonathan Gennick

The art of making small talk in social situations is one that did not come easily or naturally to me. Even in elementary school I would notice that some people could sit down to the lunch table and almost instantly be engaged in conversation with everybody around them. What's more, the conversation would drift from topic to topic in ways that I seldom could follow. Just when a topic got interesting and I was ready to dive in deeply with a comment, suddenly the group was talking about something else. I was always a half-step off.

In business, it's helpful to have a few tricks for starting conversations. One of my favorite ways to begin a conversation is with a question. If you ever catch me manning the Apress booth at a conference like PASS, the question you're most likely to get hit with is, do you have any of our books? It's a logical question that usually leads to some back-and-forth conversation about specific books and what's good and bad about them.

My question is a good conversation starter, but it's sincere too. I truly want to know what readers like and don't like about our books. I want to know which topics resonate with our audience and which do not. I'm hungry for help, really, in doing my job better.

I might ask other questions, too. Sometimes a company name will strike me as interesting. Other times I see names of cities that I've visited or lived in. Questions are a great way to get a conversation rolling. But be sincere. Don't just show interest. Be interested.

Track Your Progress

Remember that checklist? Good, because you need it in order to chart your progress over the coming weeks. As a DBA, a lot of your work is done behind the scenes. In fact, people will often wonder what it is you do all day, since much of your work is never actually seen by the end users. Your checklist will serve you well when you try to show people some of the tangible results that you have been delivering.

No matter how many people you meet and greet in the coming weeks, unless you can provide some evidence of tangible results to your manager and others, people will inevitably wonder what it is you do all day long. If your initial checklist shows that you have twenty-five servers, six of which have data and logs on the C: drive, and two others that have no backups at all, it is going to be easy for you to report later that your twenty-five servers now have backups running and all drives configured properly.

In the end, it is not your effort that people will remember. It is the end result. Make certain you keep good track of your progress so that the facts can help provide people a way to understand exactly what you have been delivering.

Get Proactive

Now that a lot of your research is complete, you should have a very clear picture about what you are up against in your new environment. As time goes on, you will be establishing your own identity in your new role. Most DBAs will fall into one of two categories: *Mr. Right* or *Mr. Right Now*.

Which one of the following would best describe how you handle your work tasks or how you want to be perceived?

> *Mr. Right Now*: This is the guy that is always available to solve any problem. He is very visible, everyone knows his name, and everyone knows what he does. He fixes things. It doesn't matter what time of the day or night, he is always there. When there is a problem—any problem—you call Mr. Right Now and he finds a way to solve that problem. He rarely fails to deliver and everyone praises his hard work and effort. However, whenever he solves a problem, he solves it just enough to move on to the next emergency.

> *Mr. Right*: This is the guy that you rarely see. When there is a problem, he pokes his head around the corner, but since there are few problems, people never really know that he is around. In fact, people often ask, "So, what is it you do around here?" But when Mr. Right solves a problem, he solves it for good, making sure that he never has to touch that server again to address that issue. Then, he proactively does that same fix against the rest of his servers before they experience a similar issue, thereby solving problems before they happen.

Which one would you rather be? Would you rather be the guy that is very visible and that the end users love because he is always there to fix things? Or would you rather be the guy that people rarely see and have no idea what you do for a living?

How about you answer this question: Which one (Mr. Right or Mr. Right Now) would you consider to be a junior DBA, and which a senior DBA?

> **TIP:** Being able to fix things does not make you a senior DBA. You become a senior DBA by making certain that things do not break in the first place.

While Mr. Right Now may be getting slaps on the back from the end users for all of his efforts, the ultimate question must be asked: is he fixing problems that are being caused by his fixing of an earlier problem?

There are two reasons for someone to be a Mr. Right Now. The first is that there are far too many problems at the onset of their tenure and they are going to be fighting a long battle to get all of the fires under control. The second reason is that they are a junior-level administrator who knows just enough to fix the current issue.

Mr. Right, however, is the guy that not only puts out the fires as they happen, but also has the knowledge and experience to put controls into place to make certain that the problems are less likely to happen again. So, they not only know enough to fix the current issue, but *they know enough to solve the root cause of the problem*. The solutions they put in place do not complicate the environment; they help to lessen their workload.

As you start your new role, there is a very good chance that you will need to be Mr. Right Now for an extended period of time, even if you are at a senior level. It could be the case that there is way more work than one person can handle. Of course you have your checklist and are well organized, so you know where to focus you efforts first. But as you go down that checklist, you need to keep thinking about solutions, as opposed to a quick fix.

Over time, you really want to be Mr. Right, and have your environment configured in such a way that it practically heals itself. And do not despair if you feel that you are losing out on an opportunity to show people how valuable you are to the company. Indeed, as you continue to configure your environment and are proactive in heading off potential trouble, you will find you have more time to be visible in different ways.

> **TIP:** Work smarter, not harder. Find ways to be proactive in solving issues.

Would you rather be stuck in a server room all weekend or be helping someone learn to write better T-SQL code? Would you rather be rebooting boxes as quickly as possible during the business day as you troubleshoot some issue, or would you rather be helping someone in finance understand how to configure and build their own reports using SSRS? Trust me, there are plenty of ways for you to show your value without having to run around the place as if it were on fire.

Back in college we were always told to study smarter, not harder. The same principal applies here: work smarter, not harder.

Chapter 3

Some Basics

You have your checklist in hand, you are meeting with people every day, and you are slowly bringing your environment under control. As you meet more and more people, you find that they appear to be speaking in code; their use of acronyms is astounding. Even more astounding is that they expect you to understand the acronyms right from the start.

This chapter will cover some of the technical basics you will be expected to be familiar with. After reading this chapter you should be more familiar with the acronyms you might be hearing frequently, such as RAID, SAN, HA, and DR, and even what DBA means to some people.

> **TIP:** No one person knows everything. Do not be afraid to tell someone that you have not heard of something that they are talking about. The best DBAs ask questions, even basic questions, to quench their thirst for knowledge.

In this chapter we will discuss the following:

1. RAID

2. Storage area networks (SANs)

3. High availability options

4. Disaster recovery (DR)

5. Why networks are like bathrooms

6. The meaning of "DBA"

7. Why you get all the blame

8. How to politely be right

Introduction to RAID

Probably the most important hardware concept you need to be familiar with is RAID, which stands for *redundant array of inexpensive disks*. RAID is essentially about different ways of storing data twice, or more than twice, on different disks. I'm oversimplifying just a bit, but a core goal of RAID is to let you survive losing a disk without also losing any of the data that was on that disk.

The redundancy part of RAID is what allows us to survive the loss of a drive. There are different ways to provide redundancy, and I'll cover those in this chapter.

Understanding different RAID configurations is going to save your bacon on more than one occasion. Different RAID configurations are called for in different situations. They can be used to improve performance as well as protect against disaster.

Why Is RAID So Important?

Consider most home computer systems that are bought from a national superstore chain. They come with more than enough memory, have more than enough processing power, and have lots of disk space. The one thing they don't come with is a backup (or external) drive. And why would you want one of those? Users need those to protect their important files, such as e-mails, pictures of the cats, and all their favorite web links.

Many homeowners don't think about backups. They go on merrily for years, adding their financial data, their photographs, and their collections of e-mail and iTunes music to their hard drives. Then one day they learn the hard way about hard drive failure. Their hard drive fails, their computer won't boot, and they lose everything.

What about servers—do they come with extra disks? Usually, yes, servers are ordered with extra disks. Depending on the model of the server, you will have a different number of options and disks available. The primary reason for extra disks, besides the need for disk capacity, is to protect yourself through the utilization of RAID in the event of a hard disk failure.

For example, Figure 3–1 shows one possible RAID configuration. In Figure 3–1, three hard drives are tied together to appear as one. The same data gets written to all three drives. Because the three drives are mirror images of each other, we can trash one of the drives and still have access to our data on the other two. We can even trash two drives, leaving just one good one.

CAUTION: Do not rely solely on raid to avert disasters. RAID is not backup. When a user deletes a record, it's instantly deleted on all drives. You still need backups to recover from small problems like these, as well as major disasters like server failures, datacenter outages, and natural disasters.

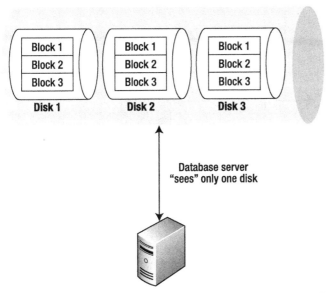

Database server
"sees" only one disk

Figure 3–1. *One path to redundancy is writing the same data to many drives.*

RAID for Performance

You can also utilize RAID to improve performance. Knowing how to do that can be helpful when trying to performance tuning queries. It will also serve you well when you go through your initial checklist and start to gather baseline information on the configuration of your servers.

SQL Server is very much an input/output (I/O)–intensive system. That means that the faster you can read and write data to and from your disks, the faster your response times will be. You can use RAID to increase your I/O throughput by taking advantage of *striping* your data across several disks at once.

For example, a traditional hard disk has a little arm inside of it that moves back and forth every time you want to read and write data. Well, let's say you had to do 100 read and 100 write operations, and each one took 1/100th of a second. How long would that take on one disk? Two seconds. Now, let's say you configured RAID as shown in Figure 3–2.

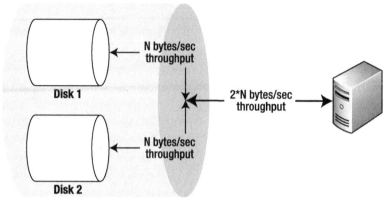

Figure 3–2. *A RAID configuration to improve performance by striping*

Now you have two little arms moving back and forth across two disks at the same time. You would still have your two hundred operations to perform, but they would be done on two drives simultaneously. Each individual drive would get half the work. Your overall time would be reduced from two seconds to one second.

Another method for improving performance would be caching. Most RAID controllers allow for some amount of data to be stored in cache. The idea would be to cache as many nonsequential requests as possible in order to batch them together and send them as a sequential request to the hard drives.

RAID for Fault Tolerance

RAID uses two methods to provide for fault tolerance: mirroring and parity. Mirroring is exactly what it sounds like: you have two (or more) copies of your data on two (or more) different disks. the scenario in Figure 3–1 is a mirroring scenario.

> **NOTE:** Mirroring is most commonly thought of in terms of two drives mirroring each other. However, there is nothing stopping you from mirroring across more than two drives.

Parity occurs when you add extra data called *parity data* to one of your disks, which can then be used to reconstruct your real data should one disk fail. The advantage of the parity approach is that you save on disk space. Figure 3–3 shows how one byte of parity data can protect two bytes of real data.

Data Byte #1

1 0 1 0 0 0 1 1

Data Byte #2

0 0 1 1 0 0 0 1

XOR
Operation

Parity Byte

1 0 1 0 0 0 1 1

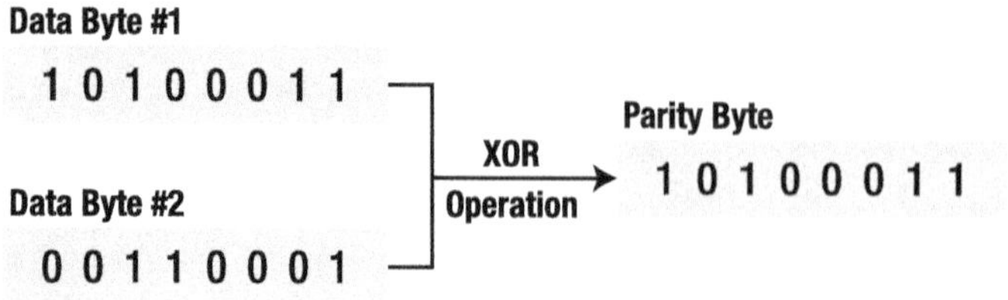

Figure 3–3. *One byte of parity data can protect two bytes of real data.*

The parity approach to RAID is a good thing, unless you are concerned about performance. There's a negative impact on performance, because writing that extra bit of parity information each and every time will add additional overhead.

Let's examine several different RAID levels that use different combinations of mirroring and parity to achieve protection and speed. I don't discuss every possible RAID level, just the ones you are likely to encounter as a DBA.

RAID 0

This level is commonly called *disk striping,* and the result is often referred to as a *striped set* of disks. Your data gets divided into chunks (or blocks) and distributed across all the disks in the array in a fixed order. Figure 3–4 illustrates the approach.

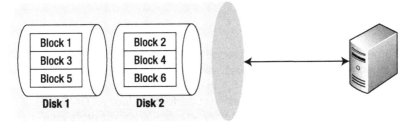

Figure 3–4. *An example of a RAID 0 configuration*

RAID 0 will increase performance as the operations can all be performed at the same time independently from one another, as noted earlier. The drawback is that any piece of data is on only one disk, because the data was divided across all of the disks evenly. In the event of a drive failure, all of the data that was on that disk is permanently lost. In fact, it's worse: lose one drive and you've effectively lost all data in the array. The only way to recover from a drive failure in a RAID 0 array is to restore the entire array from the last backup. Therefore, RAID 0 does not make a good choice for SQL Server storage. It is worth noting that RAID 0 does not provide fault tolerance, nor does it provide redundancy.

RAID 1

This level is more commonly called mirroring. It's the scenario illustrated earlier in Figure 3–1. Your data is simply written to at least two different places at the same time, creating one or more copies of your data on a separate disk. In the event of a drive failure, the array is still completely available because at least one other copy of the drive is still online and functional.

RAID 5

This level is also known as striping with parity. It is very similar to RAID 0, with one additional disk needed to hold the parity bit that gets striped across all disks. Figure 3–5 illustrates an example configuration. Without a doubt, RAID 5 is a favorite RAID level, and I have seen it used by many administrators.

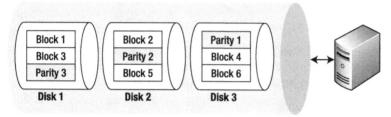

Figure 3–5. *Example RAID 5 configuration*

The reason for RAID 5 being so well liked is that if one disk fails, you simply have to add in a new disk (before a second disk fails; otherwise, you lose *everything*) and the array will rebuild itself. Sounds nice, huh? While RAID 5 can offer better performance than RAID 1, the overhead for that parity bit means it will not perform as well as RAID 0. But you do get fault tolerance with RAID 5, and that is why so many administrators love using RAID 5 over anything else.

BATTLE AGAINST ANY RAID 5?

by Jonathan Gennick

Love for RAID 5 isn't universal. Frustrated DBA James Morle created a tongue-in-cheek group known as the BAARF Party in 2003. The goal of The BAARF Party is to battle against any and all RAID 5. You can visit the web site and read the arguments at the following URL: http://miracleas.com/BAARF/BAARF2.html.

You may or may not agree with the BAARF Party—so far, I've chosen to keep an open mind—but some of the papers hosted on the BAARF Party's site are well thought out, and are worth the time to read.

RAID 1+0

This level is commonly known as mirroring with striping, and is sometimes referred to as RAID 10 or even RAID 1/0. You would configure a striped set (RAID 0) and then mirror them (RAID 1) onto a similar striped set. Figure 3–6 shows how that might look.

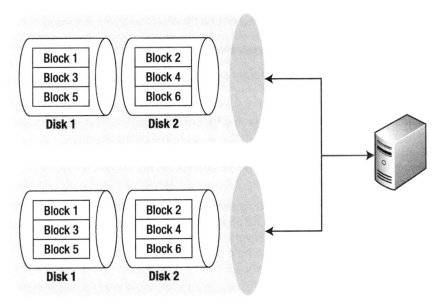

Figure 3–6. *RAID 1+0 mirroring a striped set of drives*

The RAID 1+0 level offers the highest performance of any RAID level. It provides fault tolerance, too. And it costs more money, because you need twice as many disks.

Which RAID Level Do You Want?

It depends, of course. Do you want your data to stay online when one drive fails? Most people do, but perhaps you do not. In that case, RAID 0 is for you! No need to worry about parity or mirroring, just configure your disks as one big striped set and be done with it.

What about performance and costs? Most people care about them as well, and chances are you care, too. But when it comes to SQL Server, you will find that no one RAID level is going to suit your every need. Wait a minute . . . do you know what those needs are yet? Well, let's discuss them in their simplest view.

Your Needs

You really only have three basic needs:

- Placement of your database data files
- Placement of your transaction log files
- Placement of your tempdb database files
- Placement of your database backups

OK, that's four needs, but that's it, really. Your data files should be placed on one drive or set of disks (array), your transaction log files should be placed on a separate drive or set of disks, your tempdb files should be placed onto a third set, and your backups should be stored either on a fourth set or on a different server altogether (which is often recommended).

Each item in the preceding list leads to a different set of needs. In a perfect world with bottomless budgets and hardware designed specifically for database servers, you would be able to configure everything with RAID 10. Your server's operating system files would go on one array, and your pagefile would go on a different array, as well as your data, your transaction logs, and your tempdb files. That would be five different arrays, configured as RAID 10, meaning you would need (at a minimum) twenty hard drives. In case you are wondering, that is a lot of drives. Most servers do not come with twenty hard drive bays.

But do you really need all of that? I have thousands of databases under my care right now, and 99 percent of them would perform just fine with RAID 5 for data, transaction logs, and tempdb. But there are a handful of systems that do need some extra care and attention. And when the time arises for you to help performance tune a system, it is going to benefit you if you just stick to the basics.

> **NOTE:** Tom's comment here about many systems performing just fine on RAID 5 arrays fits my own experience. It's why I haven't been able to quite bring myself to drink the BAARF Kool-Aid. – Jonathan Gennick

The biggest thing for you to recognize when troubleshooting is where you are feeling the pressure. Is it in your tempdb? Then put your tempdb on a RAID 10, if possible. Is it your transaction logs? Put your transaction logs onto a different RAID 10 set, if possible. If not, then go with a RAID 1 for your transaction logs. Is it your data files? Your data should also go onto yet a different set of RAID 10, but if that is not possible, then go with RAID 5 for your data.

The bottom line is this: know the difference between these RAID levels as well as which ones you want to use. That knowledge will be a benefit when you are helping to architect the design of any system.

The ABCs of SANs for DBAs

By now you should have the concept of RAID safely under your belt to the point that you could sit down with a member of your server team and talk a bit of shop. If you did, you will probably find that most of your servers will not have enough drive bays for all the different flavors of RAID that you might desire. You may even find yourself asking for different RAID configurations that result in conversations around external storage . . . and then someone, somewhere, will mention the following: SAN.

SAN stands for *storage area network*, and will either be the most wonderful thing you can possibly imagine (high probability) or a nightmare (not likely, but possible). The concept behind a SAN is quite simple: bundle together hundreds of physical disks, partition them out in logical units (called LUNs), and connect your servers to the LUNs for their storage. Figure 3–7 shows how one SAN can serve many servers.

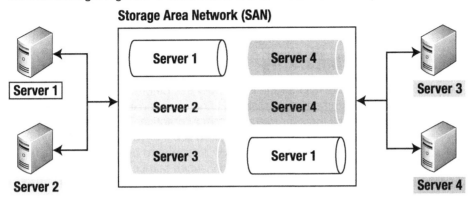

Figure 3–7. *Drives in a SAN can be assigned to many servers as needed.*

This way, if you needed to add additional storage to a server, it would be as easy as assigning some additional LUNs. In fact, most of the time, all your SAN administrator is going to ask you is, "How much space do you need now, Bob?" No need to swap out smaller drives for larger ones and let your RAID controller rebuild your array. Sounds wonderful, right?

Maybe.

Let's imagine for a moment that you are the SAN administrator. You have hundreds of disks bundled together into LUNs. Which RAID level would you use for all these disks? If you answered RAID 5 for its cost-effectiveness and large storage volume, then you may have a future in SAN administration when your DBA days are over.

Chances are your SAN is indeed configured with RAID 5. If you recall, RAID 5 is not always ideal for a database server. Don't panic: when used correctly in a SAN, RAID 5 arrays may not be ideal, but they can still be good enough.

Why RAID 5 Might Work for You

The first reason not to fear is that SAN controllers have built-in cache: memory that serves as a buffer between your server and its storage arrays. Whenever SQL Server issues writes to your drives, they're considered committed as soon as the data enters the SAN controller's cache. When configured correctly, that cache is faster than any drive arrays, whether they're RAID 5 or RAID 10. While your SAN may be at RAID 5, your data is not going to disk directly; it gets dumped into cache first and then goes to disk. Your queries do not wait for it to get to disk; they think it is already there when in fact it is actually still in cache. You see no performance issues until such time as you would actually fill your cache, in which case you have performance issues *everywhere*, not just on one server.

The second reason you should not panic is because you may have not seen any actual performance problem yet. Just because your SAN may be at RAID 5 is not enough reason to raise the hairs on your back. No sir, you had better be able to provide some proof that you are seeing performance issues that could be related to SAN performance.

The Lost Art of Benchmarking

The only way to find out for certain if storage is a bottleneck before a server goes into production is to do some benchmarking. One thing I find common in most shops these days is that fact that benchmarking is far from a common practice. People tend to slap things together, throw them into production, and wait to see if anyone screams. If you want to make the leap to being Mr. Right, then you will be wise to benchmark some of the more important processes in your shop. That way, when someone says, "This is slow," you can quickly reference the latest benchmark to determine if it really is slow or if it is just perception.

The first question you need to ask you SAN administrator when troubleshooting possible SAN performance issues is, "What is the expected I/O throughput for our SAN?" Get whatever details you can, and then go back to your cube and start gathering your own metrics. Then compare to see if the expected throughput is close enough to the observed. If not, now you can go back to the SAN administrator with some actual facts.

Believe me, that will get you a lot more traction than making a blanket statement such as, "We would like to have some space on the SAN carved out in RAID 10 for our tempdb." Unless you have proof that there is a performance issue, your SAN administrator is not going to be compelled to start carving out different RAID levels, even if you know what works best for SQL Server.

> **TIP:** The more benchmarking and testing you perform, the more control you have over your environment.

Your SAN could indeed be a performance bottleneck, and it may be very difficult for you to troubleshoot. Much in the same way that people will blame a database server because it is a big black box they do not understand, I have seen some DBAs be frustrated because their SAN is also a big box that they do not understand. The best advice I could give to you is to think of your SAN as being a constant. It should serve up a standard I/O throughput. It should allow for you to dynamically add space to a server when needed. It should be the same for each server. And that means you can perform some benchmarks on different servers, assume that the SAN performance should be equal, and take your results to the server team to discuss the discrepancies. It may indeed be the SAN, but it could also be something else.

NOT A CONSTANT, BUT A VARIABLE!

by Brent Ozar

Hmm—I tell people the opposite. Assume the SAN is a variable. The SAN team can change it without warning. You can get new neighbors that share your drives, you can have switch failures, and so forth. All these things can change your performance without warning. Perhaps the point is to test to ensure that your SAN remains a constant like it is supposed to, and so that you are alerted when it ceases to be a constant due to some unknown change by an unthinking SAN administrator.

It's All About the Spindles, Baby

If the SAN creates a performance bottleneck, then one discussion you will want to have is about the spindles. A *spindle* is a SAN administrator's slang for an individual drive that is combined together with other drives to make arrays. For example, you could have ten disks in an array, build five logical volumes on those ten disks, and each volume would have ten spindles. But if two or more of those volumes are put under stress, then all ten spindles are under stress. In an ideal configuration, your SAN would have as many spindles as possible and a minimal chance for resource contention.

Want to have some fun? Go and ask your SAN administrator this question: "If my current LUNs were converted into physical disks, how many spindles would I have allocated?" If the number is low, then you may have cause for concern. Again, that is why I stress the importance of benchmarking.

While SANs may be great, it is not all unicorns and rainbows. One of the drawbacks to SAN storage is that it can be unpredictable. For example, what if you are doing all of your database backups at the same time of day and week on your SAN? Chances are you will flood the cache and cause issues everywhere. Now imagine that it is not your backup process but an end user that decides to bulk load 20GB of data that causes performance issues on other servers that are sharing disks within the same LUNs.

One last thing to note is that your SAN may use replication, automatically sending all data from one SAN to another SAN in a different city, for high availability and/or DR purposes. Even if that is the case, you still need to be taking regular database backups. Do not let anyone try to convince you that SAN replication eliminates the need for regular database backups. About the only thing sillier would be if they said that RAID 5 eliminated the need for a database backup. It is not true, and it will only take one disaster (which will be your last disaster, by the way) for everyone to understand why the database backups were necessary. Furthermore, tools like SAN replication and RAID should still only be one part of your high availability strategy.

High Availability Options

You know enough basics on storage, but you have to worry about more than just storage to make certain your systems are always available. Keeping a database online despite problems like server crashes, OS freezes, and hardware failures is called *high availability (HA)*. As the DBA, you are going to be held responsible for making certain your database servers are always available, *even if you have nothing to do with the apparent outage*. You read that correctly. Your end users see you as the face of availability. Should the server be down because someone decided to unrack it by mistake, it will be your phone that rings, not the guy in the server room using your box as a new paperweight.

There are four major groups of HA options that you should be familiar with when having group discussions. They are clustering, log shipping, replication (both SQL and SAN), and database mirroring. Each one has advantages and disadvantages when compared to the others. The best advice I could give you is this: *there is nothing permanent except change*. What I mean by that is that you can spend a lot of time and money designing the perfect HA solution for your shop only to find that in 18 months your design is no longer adequate. Therefore it is best to keep in mind all available options and how to be flexible enough to move things around, if necessary.

> **TIP:** HA is HA and DR is DR. They are very different things. Remember that.

One last note before we continue: *HA does not mean the same thing as DR*. You systems can be highly available, but have no ability to recover from a disaster. Likewise, your system can be configured to recover from a disaster, but during recovery your systems may not be available. Please keep this in mind during your conversations. At some point you will run into a person who feels that HA is more important than DR. They will be wrong, and you will do your best to help them understand that your jobs depend more on recovering from a disaster than availability.

The topics we discuss next are mostly with an eye toward HA options, but some of them can double as both HA and DR solutions. You will need to decide which ones work best for your shop.

Clustering

One of the more expensive options with physical servers is the notion of *clusters*. In order to build a cluster, you first build your primary server (or *node*), which has a defined set of shared disks (called a *resource group*). Sharing disks between multiple nodes does not require a SAN, but having a SAN can make your life a little easier. You then add nodes to the cluster, with each node being defined to that same resource group. The entire cluster appears on your network as a single server instance, but it is really made up of multiple server instances. You will hear talk of primary nodes, secondary nodes, or failover nodes; all that talk amounts to fancy words for a server instance.

Figure 3–8 provides an example of a four-node cluster. The arrangement may at first glance appear similar to that in Figure 3–7. The difference is that all four nodes in the cluster share access to the same set of database disks. Furthermore, the outside world sees the cluster as a single database instance.

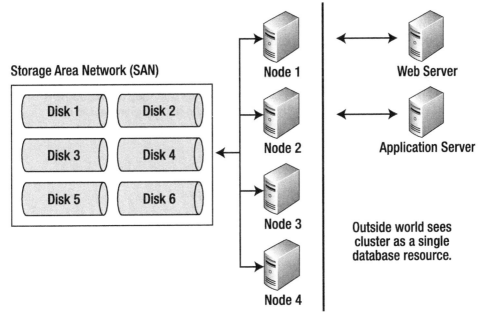

Figure 3–8. *A four-node cluster built around shared disks*

The reason clusters can be so expensive is because they typically require a lot of additional hardware like a SAN, and each node in the cluster needs to have very similar hardware. However, with virtualization you can look to use clusters with virtual servers and reduce your costs. You can even find some third-party software applications that help you to failover your virtual instances during times of peak usage, which will (in theory) help to increase your availability (often called *uptime*).

If this all sounds too good to be true, that's because it is too good to be true. There simply must be a downside to clustering, even on virtual servers, right? Absolutely.

Many times I have had the opportunity to load software onto a cluster. And despite the vendor assuring me that I only need to load their software onto the primary node, I will often find their software not working should the cluster fail over to a different node. Historically you will find horror stories relating to the application of SQL hotfixes and service packs to the primary node, and their failure to work on the other nodes. And while each version of SQL and server OS helps to reduce those headaches, you should be aware that they can still happen.

The other downside to the use of clusters is the increase in the number of servers that your shop needs to administer. While having three nodes sounds like a great way to achieve HA, it may not sound so great to the people that need to administer those instances and apply things like service packs. Believe me, administrators enjoy having a weekend off every now and then, same as everyone else.

Need more downsides to clusters? How about the amount of time it takes for the failover to happen? Depending on your configuration it can take less than a minute to several minutes. And what about those transactions and connections in flight during the failover? Will they see an interruption in service? Probably, so your application had better be able to handle such an event; otherwise, your phone will ring off the hook the minute people perceive there is an issue.

Need more downside? Well, how about that clusters do not protect you from a disk failure? If you are going about setting up clusters and think that they are a good DR strategy, then you are looking Mr. Murphy right in the face and laughing at his laws.

Log Shipping

Log shipping is a traditional method of HA, allowing for you to maintain your data in two (or more) places at the same time. The idea is quite simple:

1. Do a backup of your transaction log on your production server.

2. Copy that backup file to another server.

3. Restore that backup file to another server.

And there you go—you now have a database (see Figure 3–9) that should look just like the database that went offline for whatever reason. Well, close enough to the database that went offline. I mean, how often are you doing those transaction log backups? Every minute? Five minutes? Ten? Fifteen?

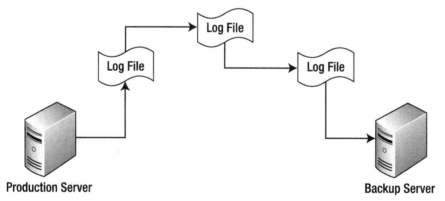

Production Server   **Backup Server**

Figure 3–9. *A log-shipping scenario*

Just how long would you be able to go without data? Would it be acceptable to tell your end users that they would be without their data for the past ten or fifteen minutes? And if you did transaction log backups every minute, are you certain they would complete in that minute? Depending on the usage and activity, you could find your transaction logs taking longer than one minute to complete their backup, meaning it would take some time to do the file copy, and then longer than a minute to do the restore. What does that mean for the jobs that keep trying to do the backups and restores every minute?

They fall behind, that's what it means. And if they fall too far behind, you will find yourself having to reinitialize everything from scratch. And depending upon the size of the files and databases involved, that could make for a long afternoon and evening.

But for a lot of people, log shipping is the way to go. Log shipping doesn't require a SAN or identical hardware on each server involved. A lot of vendors will recommend log shipping as a way to achieve HA with a fairly low amount of overhead. You do not necessarily save on costs when compared to clusters, but you do save on overall administration costs, because things like service packs and hotfixes are easier to implement, as well as installation of vendor software.

Be mindful that log shipping requires manual intervention. Unlike clustering, which can provide you with an automated failover, log shipping requires a human to get involved and to manually get the backup server up and running as a production server.

Replication

You will often be involved in conversations about replication. My first word of caution is to make certain that everyone understand what type of replication is being discussed. You have two main types of replication to be concerned with: SQL replication and SAN replication. They are not the same thing—in fact they are very different, and can exist together or separately depending on your needs.

SAN replication is simply a way your shop has configured the SAN to accommodate for moving bits of data from point A to point B. This is done primarily for HA purposes, but you will find someone who thinks it is also being done for DR purposes. Depending on how the SAN replication is configured, it most certainly is an HA option and is possibly a DR option. For example, if you have two sites and are doing SAN replication from site A to site B, then you certainly have an HA scenario configured. However, when an event happens that affects both site A and site B, both SANs will go down. Your HA is clearly going to be out of the water, and so will your DR unless you are also replicating to a third site.

I can hear people now saying that they can recover from tape, so technically they have a DR solution in place. And I will tell them the same thing I am telling you right now: *then your tape backups are your DR solution, not your SAN replication*. I hope that helps clear up the confusion.

As for SQL replication, you get your choice of flavors. Each one is unique from the rest, and each appropriate according to your particular needs. You should have a cursory knowledge of the different types and when it might make sense to deploy. Your environment and the nature of the requirements you are given will be your primary decision factors when selecting a mode of SQL replication.

Before we even get started, a quick overview of replication terminology is in order. Many of the terms used (publisher, subscriber, distributor) are used in the publishing industry, and thus the publishing industry is often used to describe replication concepts. So the term *publisher* means exactly what you would expect: someone who publishes information, like a newspaper. A *distributor* would be someone who distributes the newspapers to the people who are *subscribers*. Simple enough? Great, now let us have a look at the different types of SQL replication.

Transactional Replication

Transactional replication is when transactions committed at the publisher are then replicated and committed at the subscriber. This makes no sense in terms of newspapers or magazines, so think of this as if you were reading the online version of your local newspaper. If someone makes a change to the articles on the web site, you will see the changes the next time you refresh your browser.

When would you want to use this type of replication? Often the answer has to do with systems that have a high volume of transactions and the need for low latency, and the fact that one of your subscribers is a not a Microsoft SQL Server. Also, the subscribers in a transactional replication topology are usually considered to be read-only, but it is possible to allow for subscribers to make changes to data that are then pushed back to the publisher.

Transactional replication makes sense when you have a server that is not SQL Server, or when you have the need for more than one subscriber. If you only have one subscriber and you only have SQL Server database servers, then you should go with database mirroring instead, as discussed later in the chapter. But take into consideration the scope of the changes you want replicated. With database mirroring, all transactions are mirrored and thus replicated, but with transactional replication, only those transactions marked for replication will be replicated.

Merge Replication

This might be the biggest beast of all replication technologies. Changes at both the publisher and subscribers are merged together through the use of triggers. Think of a newspaper needing to publish the evening news that has ten reporters in the field updating stories. Now let's say that two reporters are covering the same story and try to publish different versions. Which version will get written? How would you resolve the conflicts?

Merge replication is not for the faint of heart. When this replication breaks, you had better have a method in place to put it back together again. There can be a lot of administrative overhead with merge replication. So why would anyone want to use this?

Most often I see it used when you have disconnected users from a central publisher. Often times you will see the example of having members of a sales team in the field visiting clients. Their mobile devices and laptops are not always connected, but they may be gathering data. When they do connect to the network, they want their data to update accordingly. Conflicts can (and will) arise if another sales representative tries to update the same data.

This replication topology should only be used if you have the need for many disconnected clients to connect back to the main office. If that is a requirement for your shop, then merge replication may be the answer. I would rather eat shards of broken glass than implement merge replication, but that's just me. Some people make a great living eating broken glass at carnivals. You should choose your own path in life.

Snapshot Replication

Snapshot replication requires less administrative overhead than the other two forms of replication. Just as it sounds, a snapshot of the database is taken and replicated as a whole to a subscriber. This is very useful when you have data that changes infrequently. Perhaps you might need to update your list of available products to your sales team a few times a year. When the sales representatives connect to your network, a snapshot of your data can be pushed out to them so they see all the new products.

Be careful using snapshot replication on very large data sets. You can easily cause network issues if you were to decide to push a 100GB snapshot out to 100 subscribers in the middle of the day.

If you do not have the multi–server platform requirements that would force you into transactional replication, and if you do not want the hassles of merge replication, then snapshot replication may be the right solution for your shop. While snapshot replication is the easiest type to manage, there's another method of moving data around that requires even less work and time.

Database Mirroring

Recently I was asked to explain database mirroring in the simplest terms possible. About the only thing I could think to say was the following story:

Long ago, in ancient times, in the time before time, people were asked to make copies of their work. This led to some very interesting inventions throughout history, most notably the printing press, the polygraph, and ultimately the modern day copy machines that became a big hit at holiday office parties. But as society progressed to the point where deliverables were measured in fractions of a second as opposed to days or weeks, these archaic methods were no longer good enough. More and more demand was placed upon people to deliver the same piece of information into many different places all at the same time without any loss of service.

Soon a great battle took place between two giant beasts named Cluster and Log Shipping, who had easily beaten down the inferior SQL Replication in a pay-per-view event two months prior. Cluster and Log Shipping battled for years, neither giving an inch to the other, until such time that they were both badly beaten, weakened, and barely able to stand.

At the time of SQL Server 2005's release, a great hero rose from the ashes of Cluster and the ruins of Log Shipping. The hero's name was Database Mirroring, and promised that everything was going to be different. Database Mirroring promised real-time synchronization of your data without the hassle of log shipping. Database Mirroring promised faster failover without the need for a cluster. In short, Database Mirroring promised the best of all other technologies, with none of the shortcomings, and even brought along a witness to attest to its abilities.

And there you have it. Database mirroring looks to give you the very best in HA by combining all of the good in other tools and none of the bad. However, there is one tiny little thing that makes database mirroring not as perfect as people may think: you only get one mirror.

Oh sure, you can go to a clothing store and stand in those fancy mirrors that let you see parts of your body you didn't even know existed. Well, database mirroring gives you one mirror, no more. So, if you have the need to mirror your data to more than one location, then you need a different solution. You could, if so desired, configure your mirror and also configure log shipping to other servers. But the one mirror itself will not provide that option for multiple servers.

Other than that one issue, database mirroring is a fine alternative to clustering, log shipping, and replication. It truly does offer a wonderful HA solution that will satisfy the HA requirements for many shops. In fact, asynchronous mirroring *could* be used for DR purposes, which is important as you begin to plan for what to do when disaster strikes.

Disaster Recovery Planning

DR planning is essential; not only for your job security, but for the entire company's existence. You can do a quick search on the Internet regarding the number of companies that have gone out of business simply due to their failure to plan for a disaster. Most commonly you will find companies that simply did not have any idea about the need to recover their data in a timely fashion. I see a lot of cases where companies go under because of something boneheaded, such as relying on RAID 5 as the only means for preventing a disaster.

> **TIP:** When it comes to DR, failure to plan is planning to fail.

You simply must plan for a disaster. No scenario is out of the question. Whenever I see a new design, I usually point to a particular section and ask, "What if that server disappears? What then?" Asking those types of questions are the only way to effectively plan for a disaster.

One of the better methods I have come across when it comes to DR planning is to simply ask the question, what will we do if . . . ? You ask the question until you reach a point where there is nothing left that you could effectively plan for.

Here is an example:

Q: What will we do if that server melts?

A: We have SAN replication and would just need to boot up the DR server.

Q: What will we do if the SAN replication stops working?

A: We would recover from tape to restore the DR server to last night.

Q: What will we do if the tapes are not good?

A: We would recover from the last known good tapes.

Q: What will we do if the DR server does not boot in a timely manner?

A: We could build another server.

Q: What will we do if there is no other server available to build?

A: We could go buy another server.

Q: What will we do if we cannot buy another server?

A: We could take the test server and use that one as production for the time being.

Now, compare that series of questions and answers to this type of DR planning:

Q: What will we do if that server melts?

A: We have the disks in a RAID 5 array; the chances of two disks failing is minimal.

Q: What will we do if two disks fail?

A: There is little chance of that happening.

Q: Um . . . OK . . . so, what will we do if that does happen?

A: Don't worry about it; it won't happen.

Sorry, but that does not leave me warm and fuzzy inside, nor should it make you feel comfortable either. Another good question to ask yourself and others would be, what are we trying to protect against? When it comes to DR, you can never ask enough questions, and never settle for an answer similar to "You don't have to worry about that, it will never happen."

GET OUT OF JAIL FREE

by Sylvester Carstarphen

One thing I like to get is written documentation—what I refer to as my "get out of jail free" card—when management insists a particular scenario will never happen.

DR Testing

If your company is wise, then it will be conducting regular DR tests. In some cases, regular DR testing is required by internal and external auditors in order for your company to retain a specific level of compliance. You should be aware of the DR tests and look to actively participate so that you can learn from each and every test experience.

Each DR test exercise gives you the opportunity to prepare your own DR test plans. These details are going to be quite valuable to you should a disaster happen. As you participate in the test exercise, you will inevitably come across some hidden nuance of your systems. For example, you may find a handful of servers that need to be booted in a particular order.

> **TIP:** Practice makes perfect. Give yourself an opportunity to succeed during a crisis by practicing the steps needed to recover.

It is also important that you have very clearly defined recovery times for your systems. While you may be pleased to know that you can have your DR servers functional in 45 minutes, that may be an unacceptable amount of time to your end users. Make certain that time objectives are clearly stated and that your actual recovery times are clearly recorded for everyone to see. Otherwise, it will be difficult to know during a real disaster whether things are going well (but it will be painfully obvious if things are going poorly).

This reference will also be handy when you are recovering from disaster. If you know your testing took 30 minutes to recover, then you can reference your earlier testing and notify your customers as to when they can expect their systems to be back online.

Carnegie Hall

There is an old joke about a young man asking for directions in New York City. He stops an older man and asks the question, "How do I get to Carnegie Hall?" The old man replies, "Practice, practice, practice." When I was coaching basketball, I would always tell my team to practice "game shots" from "game spots" at "game speed." In other words, you practice how you play, which should be all out, all the time. If you practice at half speed, you end up playing at half speed.

All of that holds true for DR preparation. You need to practice and keep your skills sharp. When was the last time you tried to recover the master database? Or, better yet, have you *ever* tried to recover the master database? Believe me, when the pressure is on during a disaster event, the last thing you want to be doing is fumbling around with manuals and pounding your fist against your monitor because you do not know how to get your instance started.

Practice recovering the master database. Try recovering the msdb database sometime as well. Spot check your backup files and do a restore to make certain you are familiar with the process. Pay particular attention to your important systems. If you do nothing else right, recovering the important systems without any problems just may be enough to save your job, so practice with those and make certain you are familiar with any subtleties that they may contain.

You simply cannot practice enough when it comes to a disaster. As a DBA, your primary responsibility is to recover the data in the event of a disaster. Therefore, it is the one thing you need to plan for and practice most often.

Networks Are Like Bathrooms

When issues arise, and *issues will always arise*, people will start to blame the pieces of their environment they know the least about. As the DBA you will find people inevitably blaming the database server for all sorts of problems. In my experience I have seen people blame the database server for a host of problems that have nothing to do with the database server. The fact is that they know the database server exists, but they don't know if it is truly the problem, so they just point their finger in your direction first.

One of the last things that anyone ever thinks about is the network. Your network has ups and downs all the time. There are lots of wires, routers, and switches that make up the backbone of your network. With so many moving parts that need to go together in order to make your systems work, it is easy to understand that issues will arise from time to time. I once read a study that said how database servers are the number one piece of infrastructure that people are ordered to troubleshoot, but over 70 percent of all issues are directly related to bad application code.

As a DBA you may sometimes find yourself blaming the network simply because you cannot possibly blame bad code all of the time. And it is fine for you to blame the network, because the network team will usually just blame management for not agreeing to buy the right equipment. But the truth is that people will often misunderstand the difference between networks and computers.

It's common to hear people in offices yell out, "The database server is down!" when the problem is something completely different. Networks are a lot like your bathroom at home.

Call a Plumber

I could not tell you the first thing about plumbing, but it would not take more than a few nights of listening to a leaky faucet before I would head down to the hardware store to start asking questions. But a leaky faucet does not mean that you have a problem with your plumbing. Likewise with database servers; if your database server crashes, that does not mean your network is offline. And if one workstation is showing signs of a problem and others are not, then chances are it is not the network either. (For the record, if one workstation has problems and others do not, the problem is not likely the database server either.) And if that workstation cannot print to a network printer, you will not solve that problem by going into the network closet.

If your faucet were to spit out some dirty water, what would you do? Probably let it run for a few minutes to see if it clears up, right? Perhaps the city was working on the water lines, and after a few minutes the issue will go away. If you cannot get to a web site or a particular network server, maybe someone is moving some cables around. People need to perform maintenance on a regular basis, and it is not practical to expect everything to be flawless all the time. Wait a few minutes and try again before sounding the alarm.

You don't have to be a plumber, however, to know that if you run out of hot water after a 5-minute shower, you are going to need to spend some money to fix the problem. And most businesses will put up with a slow network for a period of time rather than face the expense of actually fixing the problem. Having the network administrators work an extra day a week is not going to solve the problem, either.

The stuff that matters most is invisible and expensive. Beautiful faucets won't impress anybody if the entire house is running off a one-half-inch garden hose. The real backbones of your plumbing system are the water heater and the pipes running behind the walls and under the floorboard. Those pieces are hard to go back and fix later, so you don't want to make those purchasing decisions without qualified help. If you're not buying this kind of equipment on a regular basis, you don't know the ins and outs of the brands, features, and even the local regulations involved. Network hardware is the same way: the basic plumbing guidelines stay the same, but things change every year; and without help, you can end up buying gear that you can't easily replace later.

Fix It Now!

Good plumbing requires a lot of knowledge and planning. If you need to water your lawn, you can slap some hose extensions together, scatter some sprinklers around, and turn the faucet on whenever the grass starts to turn brown. But if you want to do a good job, get your lawn looking perfect, and not have to hassle with moving the sprinklers around and manually turning the faucet off and on, you have to do your homework. When it comes time to build a network, you want to research how the pipes work and what kinds of connectors to use, strike a balance between reliability and affordability, and make sure you never have to touch the equipment again. None of that is guesswork.

Even the most minor plumbing problem is perceived as an emergency. When somebody can't get hot water to take a shower, they get angry quick. They might be able to make do with cold water, but they're not happy about it, and they proceed to tell everybody they meet about what a lousy morning they're having, and how the landlord better fix it or there's going to be trouble. When a user is having a problem, they yell and pull their hair out. Problems from "I can't print on the network!" to "The database server is slow!" are all spoken with the same urgent tone of voice, and everyone will expect you to drop everything immediately.

DBA Stands For . . .

Now that you have some technical basics, let's review some professional basics. To start with, let's look at the following question:

What does DBA stand for?

Depending on whom you ask, you will get a different answer. You might respond with "database administrator," and technically you would be right. To some the answer would be "default blame accepter." And to others it could be an acronym for "don't bother asking." Keep poking around and you will find that there are many different points of view with regard to what DBAs do, what DBA stands for, and what DBAs should be doing that they are not currently doing already.

Why so many viewpoints? DBAs touch many different areas of the company in many different ways. To many end users, we are the ones that reset their passwords and the ones that fix things when the system is running slowly. As such, we are also blamed for the systems running slowly even if we had nothing to do with the design of the system (especially with vendor applications). In short, DBAs get blamed for a lot of things that they have no control over, but because they have been helpful at one point or another when troubleshooting, they are ultimately seen as the owners.

> **TIP:** No one knows what you really do, not even your boss. They only know what you do not do, or to be more precise, they only remember your failures and easily forget all your success.

Ask a developer about what a DBA does and you will be told that they are a roadblock to progress. The implementation of standards and guidelines for database usage only slows down development work. Of course, the upside is having a stabler environment, but that hardly matters to the developer screaming that they need sys admin access or else their project will be late.

With these different touch points around your role, you also have different perceptions, and you need to be aware of these perceptions so that you can make an effort to mitigate them before they drive a wedge between you and your customers. There are three things to keep in mind for all of your interactions daily.

People Will Resist Change

Change happens, it's a fact. So why do so many people resist change, despite the fact that it happens all the time? You would think that everyone would be used to having things change, and yet some people stubbornly refuse to let go.

There are three main drivers of change: people, technology, and information. In case you were not aware, as a DBA you will (most likely) be working in a division of a company called Information Technology. That title has two of the three drivers alone! Toss in the fact that *people* are employed there, and it's no wonder you will see so much change on a daily basis. To quote Alan Zimmerman, "The real problem isn't the change . . . it's people's reaction to the change."

The change cycle itself has three stages: a beginning, a middle, and an end. When change happens we can dive right into it at the beginning, while in the middle we feel tied to both our past (known) and our future (unknown) states, and at the end we finally let go of the known state, which is often something we found dependable and reliable. As people pass through these three stages, they react in different ways. Consider the following type of groups of people you may already know:

- Innovators
- Early adopters
- Early majority

- Late majority

- Late adopters

- Diehards

Probably sounds like just about everyone you know, right? And there is a good chance that those classifications apply to yourself as well, and you fall into a different class for different things. Perhaps you never upgrade to a new version of software until the first service pack is released. Sound familiar? And perhaps you are also first in line to buy the latest iPhone. In some cases you embrace change and in others you proceed with more caution.

The value that one places on the items and things most familiar to them is what will lead them to either embrace or resist change. Think about that for a moment. If you place more value on the known than the unknown, would you not also resist change? The same holds true for the end users that you support. If you propose that they start doing a lot of things differently, you had better be prepared to show them how much more valuable the future state will be than the current one.

Why do you stand in line for the new iPhone? Because you value the new model more than your current one. Why do you wait for the first service pack to be released before even considering upgrading your software? Because you value the stability of your current system more than the new version.

As a DBA you are going to be asked to lead change on a number of occasions. And, on some occasions, you won't be *asked* to lead change—you will need to get up out of your cube and do it yourself without being told. When the time comes, follow these simple guidelines:

1. Define the need from the organization's point of view.

2. Define the need from the individual (or end user's) point of view.

3. Describe the desired outcome.

4. Define a timeline.

Believe me, this will take practice. Very few people have innate soft skills that allow for them to easily get people to embrace change. But for those that do, and for those that learn them, the result is a powerful way to motivate and energize people to new places.

You should also be aware of the types of resistance behaviors. You get two flavors for that: passive and active. Passive resistance would be a person who agrees verbally to everything you say but never follows through on what they agree to, or who feigns ignorance and perhaps withholds information. Active resistance would be a person who looks to find fault and ridicules change; who manipulates and appeals to a sense of fear. If you are aware of these behaviors when dealing with people, you can head off problems long before they become bigger problems.

Having Standards and Processes Is Not a Bad Thing

It is inevitable that at some point you will be approached by someone who says they do not understand why you are doing things in a particular way. Chances are that this is a result of your having put into practice some standards that help you to provide a stabler environment. And these same people will be dumbfounded that (1) you need to have such a standard and (2) that it should really have to apply to *them*.

For example, suppose you are the new DBA in a shop that had no previous DBA. Everyone had full access to the database servers and could do whatever they wanted. To say things were a mess might be too kind. Being the good DBA that you are, you go through your checklist and find a few ways to make immediate improvements that would be of a great benefit to the entire company.

First, you go through each server and database and correctly place the data and log files on separate drives in an effort to avoid a large disaster. While getting the files moved around, you revoke the ability for anyone except yourself to create a new database. You do this because your root cause analysis of the problem led you to the conclusion that the reason there were so many databases set up incorrectly was because too many people did not understand the implications of their actions. In an effort to help them avoid hurting themselves, you make the necessary changes.

About an hour after you start revoking access, you get a phone call from a developer that cannot understand why they cannot create a database. "It's just a database—why should I call you to create one when I am capable of doing it myself?" You will resist the urge to respond with, "If you could do it yourself, then I would not have spent a week cleaning up after you like the guy following the horses on the Fourth of July," and will do your best to explain that in an effort to have a stable environment, it is best if database creation were in the hands of the few, not the many.

Try to understand that most people have a horizontal view or experience in their daily life. Developers need to get to work, log into the network, access the database server, make changes, test their changes (hopefully), and deploy changes to production. Why is that a horizontal view? Well, think of all the vertical silos they went through during the day:

- They drove to work, parked their car, and entered the building (facilities).
- They logged into the network (domain controllers, network).
- They accessed the database servers to make changes (you).
- They test their changes (get customer sign-off).
- They deploy their changes to production (you again).

You have nothing to do with their access to the building or their access to the network in general, but you do have some control over how they are allowed to make changes to the database servers. In this scenario your view is a vertical one: you are mostly concerned with your silo (database servers), and have no idea what the horizontal view looks like. And this can be a very hard thing to reconcile; you really need to work with your end users and communicate with them on a frequent basis to understand all of their pain points.

Once you start to understand that most of your end users are taking a horizontal view, it is easy to see why they might be frustrated when you start to enforce policies, guidelines, and standards. Remember that people may resist change and use this as an opportunity to lead change. Over time your soft skills will improve to the point that people will begin to trust that your actions are best for the company as a whole, and not intended as a slight to any one individual.

People Will Blame What They Do Not Understand

This one is fairly self-explanatory. People will always tend to blame something they are aware of but do not fully understand. It is only natural, right? I mean, if you think you already know everything about nine out of ten items, then your mind will focus on that tenth item and you will spend far too much time on why the tenth item is causing you so much heartache at the moment.

You will frequently be told such things as, "Our code hasn't changed in years," "Everything ran fine last night," and "You guys must have done something yesterday because now all of our stuff runs much slower." Get used to being the focus of attention for any problems with any system. Start developing some thick skin because you are going to need it, and soon.

Any time there is even one hint that something is amiss with a system, the first thing people will do is blame the database server. Despite the fact that there are many layers between their screen and the database server, your phone will be the first to ring. You will be expected to investigate the issue immediately, and you will also be surprised to see e-mails with sentences that read, "I called the DBA and they are going to fix the problem." Wait a minute! We never said there was a problem with the database server—why are you telling people we are going to fix anything? The problem could be the network, or a poor design that didn't scale, or *anything*. And yet people will fixate on the database server because (1) it is known and (2) most people do not understand how it works. And in some cases, if they get an error message such as, "Could not connect to the database" (or the word "database" is simply in the error message somewhere), people automatically assume that the problem *must* be with the database.

I have lost count of the number of times I have been told there is something wrong with the server only to find that the issue is that the person or account did not have rights to log in. Sorry, but that is not a problem with the server. And it is also not a problem with the server if you try to load 100GB of data onto a disk that only has 10GB of space free. Same for filling up a 33GB tempdb drive; the issue is not with the server, it is with inefficient code. And yet your server (and ultimately yourself) will be forced to carry the burden of fault.

That's OK, because one of the reasons you are a DBA is because you are able to carry such a burden as would crush most of your peers.

Blame vs. Credit

In the preceding section, we discussed how people tend to blame things they do not understand. Another fact that you need to get used to is that people rarely go out of their way to give you credit for the things you do or suggest should be done. I have never once come to work to be told, "Nice job last night, our batch load ran two seconds faster than expected." But if it runs two seconds longer, then you may be asked to start on a Star Trek–type Level 5 diagnostic, whatever that means.

You are going to find out quickly that the only time you get noticed is when things go wrong. Some DBAs start to think that the only way they can show value is if they are always around to fix the things that go wrong. Personally I would rather build out an environment that hums along nicely without anything ever going wrong to begin with, even if that means I will never be noticed.

If you do find yourself in the situation where you are not being noticed, then what you need to do is start building out some metrics. Start with something simple, like your database backups. Track how many backups were taken in the past week and how many backups failed. At some point, perhaps a month or two, you can use the data to report to your manager. If you have reduced the number of backup failures over time, then this report is going to help you demonstrate your value to the company in a way that did not require something to go wrong before you got noticed.

TIP: Metrics and reporting are ways for you to demonstrate your value; use them wisely.

Metrics are a wonderful way for you to build up a stable environment, report on the good work you are doing, and show value besides during a disaster. Besides tracking backups and backup failures, here are a few other good items to track over time:

- Number of databases (broken down to production, nonproduction, etc.)
- Amount of space used on disk by database files
- Amount of space used by database backups
- Amount of time taken to back up databases
- Number of database restores
- Number of new databases created

All of this information is readily available in the system databases, and will go a long way to help you make certain that people are aware of your work behind the scenes.

The Need to Be Right vs. Being Liked

Nobody will like it if you are right all the time. And everyone is going to want you to be right all the time. Good luck reconciling those two items.

People are going to come to you because they want to know the right way to get things done. It is times like that when you want to do your best to help them find the right solution. While failure to be right all of the time in such discussions is not going to have people calling for your head anytime soon, if you have the need to be right all the time, then you will find yourself having issues with coworkers.

If there is a problem (and there is *always* a problem), and your database server gets blamed (which will happen 70 percent of the time), and you tell people that it is not the database server (which will the case 90 percent of the time), and it turns out to indeed not be the database server, you do yourself no good by reminding people you were right all along.

Trust me on this one. Do not feel the need to remind people that they should have listened to you in the first place. Over time either people will gravitate toward you for your advice and experience, or they will stay away from you because they hate the feeling they get every time they run around the office yelling that the sky is falling, and you tell them to sit down and stop yelling.

Keep in mind that your approval ratings are important when it comes time for a salary review. You may be right all the time, but get ignored due to your attitude, and you will not be in line for any merit increase as a result. However, you could be well liked, almost always wrong, and find yourself moving up on the salary pay scale.

You are going to run into people you work with that either (1) want to be right themselves or (2) want you to be wrong for a change. It will happen, just as the sun will rise in the east. Do not panic when this happens; remain calm when you sense that someone else is getting worked up. The last thing you want to do is have the problem escalate. If necessary, offer to have your discussion with a neutral third party, perhaps a colleague or a manager that both of you respect. Present your case and choose your battles wisely. Sometimes there is a decided advantage in giving ground to someone, even when they are wrong.

When you give ground, it will help to demonstrate that you can be reasoned with to some degree. It may win you a few points with your colleagues as well. In fact, if you give enough ground, you will find that you may be very well liked around the office. While that may make you feel good about yourself, you need to balance your desire to be liked with your need to enforce standards and follow guidelines. It can be a difficult line to follow, but over time you will learn which battles are worth fighting.

Chapter 4

A Development Server Is a Production Server to a Developer

You are going along well, and everyone is getting along swimmingly, but have you noticed that the better you get at your job, the more you are asked to do? And have you also noticed that often developers will reach out to you only in case of an emergency on their part, and that everything is always an emergency, no matter what the server? Expect to always be in demand, especially as you get better at your job. Good DBAs are worth their weight in gold, and soon you will be no exception.

This chapter will help you to understand why you are always going to be in demand, right from the start of your career, and even more as you progress. After reading this chapter, you should develop a highly refined sense of empathy for your coworkers, or you will want to stab them in the leg with a pen more than ever. It could go either way, really, but let's hope for more of the former and less of the latter.

TIP: Please do not stab anyone, thanks.

In this chapter we will discuss the following:

1. Why developers are so needy

2. Why you need to define your service-level agreements early

3. Tips on how to better manage expectations

4. Tips on time management

5. Why Chris Hansen should be doing code reviews for your company

Why Developers Are So Needy

If you have spent any time yourself building and coding applications, you can skip this section, as you already know all the reasons why developers are so needy. If you have come from the server administration world and have fallen into database administration, then read on so that you can have a better understanding of the life on the other side of the fence. You will probably find that you have more in common with developers than you might think.

Before I became a DBA, I spent over six years as a programmer/analyst. I worked on a variety of projects during that time, some that were very high profile and others that have faded into obscurity with the passage of time. I am familiar with the demands of the job and hope this section will allow for you to become familiar with those demands as well.

Under Pressure

Developers are under pressure. In some cases, it can be a lot of pressure. They are not only building new code and enhancements for existing products, but they also have responsibility to support the products they have already built. Support issues can happen at any time of the day or night, but usually at night.

> **TIP:** Production support can result in less than an ideal number of hours of sleep for a developer. If you are not familiar with sleep deprivation, just wait, because DBAs also get to share that burden.

When systems break, the developers that built the application are the first ones to be called upon to troubleshoot. And they are not always given the luxury of time to fix things, let alone fix them correctly. Sometimes it is just easier for a developer to press a few buttons manually in order to nurse the system along, despite their desire to fix things properly. They just may not have enough time, or doing things "properly" may not be a priority. And don't be quick to blame the developer. Priorities often come from management.

As a result, developers can end up calling you in the middle of the night or stopping by your cube during the day with an urgent request for your assistance. And when they do stop by your cube, you may be surprised to hear that the nature of the emergency is not necessarily a production issue.

No, they may be having an issue with a development or even a test server. And despite its non-production status, a developer's problem can indeed be a serious problem.

See, the developer could be under pressure to finish up their project by the end of the week and the development server is not responding. Or their code could be deployed to test, but the test server is not responding and the end users are not able to conduct their testing.

As a DBA, you will often find yourself multitasking on perhaps a dozen different tasks that need your attention. But developers usually have a narrower focus, working on one or two projects at a time. Therefore, if a development server is having issues, you may hear a developer say, "I cannot do any work until you fix this." As surprising as that may sound to you, it is very true.

> **CAUTION:** No matter what the pressure, or the little amount of sleep, it is never appropriate to treat a colleague unprofessionally. Yelling, making bombastic demands, and verbal abuse is never acceptable.

Development servers are essentially production servers, because development is always moving forward. Production servers are stable entities; the code should rarely change, the systems should be integrated and working, and very little change should happen on production. But development is always moving forward, and developers are doing most of the pushing. As such, you will need to be as responsive to their development requests as you are to any production requests.

12 ANGRY DEVELOPERS, OR MORE

by Jonathan Gennick

Once I was troubleshooting a report still in development that ran slow. I decided to change a table parameter to enable parallelism in the query underlying the report. That went well. The report finished in about two-thirds the original time. I was pleased, and made the same change to the client's development system that I'd just made in my own "sandbox."

Then the phone rang.

You see, the table I had modified was fundamental to the entire system. It was at the core of just about every screen and report. What's more, the table parameter change that I'd just made caused every single query involving the table to switch from using Oracle's rule-based optimizer to using the cost-based optimizer. The change happened in real-time, and suddenly almost every query plan in the system was completely botched up.

It was only a development system, right?

Yes, but the client's development team was working long hours and late nights to get a new system ready for production rollout. They were not amused. My one small change brought an overworked team of over a dozen people to a complete halt.

Business Needs

No matter what your business, things will change. And these changes will be reflected in the systems your company maintains and builds. And those changes are built and deployed by the developers. And you should just do as you are told and not ask any questions when someone demands to be a member of the system administrator's fixed-server role.

> **TIP:** One of the sentences in the preceding paragraph is false. Can you spot which one? It is the last sentence—you should always ask why someone is requesting such access.

Your end users are demanding. They could be people sitting one row away from you or they could be on the floor of a warehouse in another country. If their systems break, they are going to let you know about it. Often these complaints will make their way to the developers first. That means you are probably going to be the last one to know about anything going on with regard to your systems. In other words, don't make plans for this weekend, because someone, somewhere is probably going to need your help with something.

These business needs are going to place additional pressures on the developers, which in turn will place additional pressures on you. It all flows downhill.

SQL Knowledge

SQL Server has a *lot* of functionality inside. Have you ever noticed how many components have the letters *SQL*? Here's a short list:

- SQL Server
- SQL Server Management Studio (SSMS)
- SQL Server Reporting Services (SSRS)
- SQL Server Integration Services (SSIS)
- SQL Server Analysis Services (SSAS)
- SQL Server Notification Services (SSNS)
- SQL Azure

And if it has the letters *SQL*, you can bet that someone will walk up to you at some point to ask you a question. And when you respond with, "No, I do not know how to wrap a notification from SSNS into an SSIS package, build a report in SSRS, and then push everything to SQL Azure," you will get a blank stare and hear the words "But aren't you the DBA?"

> **TIP:** Remember, no one person knows everything.

The answer is yes. Yes, we are the DBAs, but that does not mean we know everything about each product that has the letters *SQL*. It's the same reaction a developer has when I say, "What do you mean you need me to restore the production database from yesterday down to test so that you can get a stored procedure? Don't you have a copy of the stored procedure in your source control?"

GETTING ASKED ABOUT SQL

by Jonathan Gennick

A few years ago, I was approached about teaching a class on "SQL." I don't remember now whether it was someone who'd read my books and articles, or whether the person had simply heard that I was good at SQL. What I soon discovered though, was that the person wanted someone to teach a class not on SQL the query language, but on SQL Server the database management system. They are two different things, of course. Trust me. I am comfortable with SQL, but you do not want to see me teaching about SQL Server.

Now that we have established that SQL Server has a lot of functionality, you need to be aware that developers are going to ask you a lot of questions about various components that you have never used. That's OK—do not panic—the developers are doing their job well and are researching different ways to complete a particular task.

With all the functionality that SQL Server has to offer, developers are not only going to ask you to help them to make something work, but they are going to also expect that you can help explain why something works in a particular way. It could very well be the case that a particular component of SQL Server is working in a way that is contrary to what everyone expects. Of course, you will be expected to provide an answer for the behavior; the answer had better be found fast, and the answer better come with a solution that does not require the developer to undo months of coding. If it does, then that same developer is going to ask for you to take out a hammer and make the square peg fit into the round hole.

If such a situation comes up, you should do your best to offer the developers a handful of alternative solutions. The last thing anyone wants is for some Band-Aid solution to make its way to production. Too many times I have seen poorly designed systems deployed to production simply because a developer did not want to admit that perhaps they could have done things in a way that did not cause a slow memory leak and subsequent server reboots once a week.

Usually when that happens, they do their best to shrug their shoulder and tell you to ask Microsoft for a patch to fix the problem. After all, they don't have time to fix things right because they are under pressure to finish some other project.

Service-Level Agreements

Service-level agreements (SLAs) are a must have for any DBA. If your shop already has SLAs defined, you must take the time to review them. Knowing the defined SLAs will help you to prioritize your tasks. For example, if you have two tasks to perform, and one must be done in four hours and the other has a limit of two days, then it is easy for you to decide which one to work on first.

TIP: SLAs are good for a variety of reasons, most notably that they can help you to prioritize your current tasks.

If your shop does not have defined SLAs, then you must sit down with your manager and start discussing them. Do your best to define the SLA for groups of requests that you get most frequently, and also discuss the varying levels of environments. For example, if an end user needs a password reset in production, that should be given a priority over a password reset to the test environment. It will be hard to draw a hard line on each and every task that you receive, so it is best to classify requests in a particular category.

Some examples of categories could include the following:

- Password resets
- Database restores
- Database backups
- Creating server logins
- Creating new databases
- Performance tuning

For each of those categories you should also consider the level of environment. So production requests take precedence over anything else, right? Well, maybe. It also depends, of course, on your customer.

Being a Good Customer

While you have a duty to provide quality customer service to your end users, there is also something to be said for being a good customer. As a DBA you are working in a service profession; you provide a service for all your customers. Many of those customers are also providing a service for others. Naturally you would expect that there would be some professional courtesy extended when it comes to your level of service. Of course, you would be wrong to expect such a courtesy from everyone.

Even having an SLA defined will not stop people from demanding everything be done yesterday. Developers will want their requests filled immediately for a development server and could care less about any production issues you may be working on, or the need for you to review your dashboard reports from last night, or whether you are trying to perform some needed maintenance.

Developers typically want action; they want to see you doing something, and preferably doing what they need done at that moment. Otherwise, they assume you are not doing anything when you are not working on something specifically for them. When a developer complains that something is taking too long, then it is time for you to compare just how long it has been to the defined SLA for the task.

TIP: Keep this in mind the next time you interact with someone in a store or restaurant. If you feel yourself getting impatient because the level of service is not to your liking, ask yourself if you have been a good customer first before making your complaints known.

Communication Is Key

I have seen that a lot of frustration around tasks and their completion comes down to a simple amount of communication. I have lost count of the number of times I have seen e-mails from a customer asking for an update on the progress of a task that the DBA would know is going to take another hour or more. So why was the customer expecting something to be completed sooner? *Because they had no idea how long the request should take!*

So how do you avoid this? With communication, of course. Let's consider two scenarios for the same request.

Scenario one: A developer needs to have the latest production backup restored down to the development server. They send an e-mail to the DBA with the details, and the DBA responds back saying they will perform the restore. An hour goes by and the developer gets impatient because they haven't heard back, and after all, *it's just a database restore—how long should that take?* So the developer sends another e-mail to the DBA asking how much longer. The DBA responds and says that there is not enough space on the development server to restore the production database, so they have contacted a member of the server team to see if the drive can be expanded, and they haven't heard back from them yet. The developer is very frustrated upon hearing this and wants to know if there are any other options to have this done quickly *because they are trying to resolve a production issue.* Now, the initial request was for a restore from production to development, nothing more. Such a request would have a defined SLA of perhaps one business day. So the DBA is performing his tasks well, trying to solve the issue within the defined time frame. However, the developer is clearly expecting a different turnaround time and thus became frustrated. Likewise, the business end users, management, and just about everyone that can spell *DBA* is now displeased with the level of service from the DBAs.

Scenario two: A developer needs to have the latest production backup restored down to the development server. They send an e-mail to the DBA with the details, and the DBA responds back saying they will perform the restore. The DBA determines that there is not enough space to perform the restore and sends an e-mail back to the developer to inform them about the issue, that they are contacting the server team to ask for more space, and that once the space is added the restore itself will take about 3 hours given the size of the current production database. The developer then informs the DBA that this is more than just a routine restore and asks if there is any other option at this point. The DBA responds back that the test server has enough space and they could start the restore there after taking a backup of the current test database. The developer agrees and a minimal amount of time is lost.

Now, which scenario looks better to you, and why?

For me, I like scenario two, because it demonstrates how some extra communication can improve the service you provide to your customers. The piece of communication that is entirely in your control is your initial response to the person making the request. I like to provide them an estimate as to how long it will take for you to complete your work. You do not need to be exact, but you do need to give a rough idea. Will it take 30 minutes? An hour? Two hours? A day? This way the requestor has an idea as to what point they should send a follow up e-mail should the task not be completed; plus they can then in turn communicate the progress to their customer as well.

The other piece of communication is nothing you control, and that is the initial request. Ideally the request would have all the necessary details, including the fact that they are trying to troubleshoot a production issue. Unfortunately that is not always going to be the case. As such, you may need to solicit some additional details from the requestor—but how are you to know which details are the important ones for you to know right now? You don't, so you focus on the things you can control, and respond with the details on the actions you are going to take. That way you give the requestor the opportunity to review your actions and the timeline (the timeline is all they really care about, by the way). And if the timeline is not adequate, then they have the opportunity to make that known.

> **TIP:** Giving people the ability to review your progress helps them share in the responsibility should events turn for the worse.

I can never stress the importance of communication enough. In fact, I often use some example from my former life as a basketball coach to stress how well communication works. When my team took the floor, I always reminded them about the necessity of talking to each other while playing defense. We could be winning by twenty points and I would still remind them that they needed to be talking more. Teams that talk on defense are more engaged and more energized. It can be demoralizing to an offense to have to hear about how the defenders know exactly what play is about to be run. Just by the simple act of talking you can accomplish so much more than by remaining silent.

That respect for the power of communication is something I carry with me to corporate life as well. More communication is always better than no communication.

Managing Expectations

If you have well-defined SLAs in place, then it is easier to manage expectations, right?

Wrong. Just because you have a defined SLAs in place *does not* mean people will stop expecting you to have everything done yesterday. If someone requests a database restore and you get it done in 30 minutes, then that person is going to expect that same turnaround time for each subsequent request. A few days later you may be asked to do it again, and it will take 45 minutes because the volume of data is greater. But the customer may now expect it in 30 minutes, and will think you are performing your job poorly as compared to the other times.

How do you manage that expectation? Do you communicate every action (e.g., "I'll start it now, and e-mail when done.")? Do you configure and build a process to automagically send an e-mail when the task is complete? No matter what you decide, the key point to remember is consistency. Hopefully you will have a good customer; one that is professional enough to ask if there was any issue as to why it took 15 minutes longer today. If you are unlucky, then you will have someone just accuse you of being incompetent or unwilling to help when they needed you.

No One Cares About Effort

Better you hear this now from me than later during a performance review. The only thing that truly matters to your customers is the end result; they do not care what it takes to get there. On their end they make what they believe to be a simple request. On your end you may have to spend hours getting it done, miss dinner with your family, or cancel your weekend plans.

And no one cares about inconvenience, either. If there is the need to deploy some changes to production on a Saturday, and you do not get an e-mail until Friday afternoon at 5:00 p.m. that you are needed to work tomorrow, no one will care to hear about how you have already made plans. It just does not matter; you are expected to provide support at all times no matter what amount of notice you are given.

And there are going to be times when you are asked to come into the office on a weekend just because you *might* be needed to do something. Remember, no one cares about effort or inconvenience. What they do care about are results and perception. The fact that you may sit in your cube for 8 hours on a Saturday and end up doing nothing is better than doing nothing without being seen. And everyone will tell you that they understand it makes no sense to be asked to sit there all day and do nothing, but you have to do it anyway.

So, what are some things you can do to better manage the expectations that others will have of you as a DBA?

Let's Talk

Pure and simple, nothing beats sitting down and talking with someone. The more people get to know you, the more they will get to understand what it is you actually do for work. Along the way they will get to understand the variety of tasks you perform and even some of the difficulties you face.

If your shop has multiple offices, then it is going to be more difficult to sit down and talk with people. While it is more difficult, it is not impossible. No matter who you are talking with or where they are located, the most important thing you can do is maintain an even tone of voice.

Another tip is to learn the power of the phrase "I understand." Those two words can communicate a lot to the person you are talking with. You could be saying that you agree with them (I understand what you are saying), or you could be saying that you do not agree with them (I understand what you are saying, but I am still not convinced). The bottom line is that you can be a most agreeable person to talk with simply by using those two words.

Now imagine this conversation:

> *"Why the hell is that restore taking so long?"*
>
> *"Well, it looks like the database has grown in size. It should take another 15 minutes."*
>
> *"We need it to be finished now; why is it not done yet?"*
>
> *"I understand that you need it done quickly, and as soon as it is done I will send you an e-mail, or I can call you if you prefer."*

How could someone possibly be expecting you to do anything more for them at this point? By talking with them, you make a connection with them, show them that you are human and that the desired results are coming, and most importantly that *you understand their needs*. This might be the most important thing you could ever communicate to someone, and it is easiest to communicate when you sit down to talk.

Get Involved Early

Another way to help you manage expectations is to make certain you are involved at an early enough phase of any project. Of course, this may not always be possible—for example, if you are not somehow privy to information on new projects. In fact it is quite possible that most of the time the only way you are going to be privy to anything related to a project is when an e-mail arrives and says something to the effect of, "Please put your life on hold for the next three days starting at 6:00 p.m. tonight, thanks."

If you are able to get involved early, the benefits are tremendous. First, you will be able to voice concern over possible design flaws. This can save many hours of time later when a design that works fine for a few bits of data suddenly performs poorly when many gigabytes of data are being pumped through. Or when someone insists on using a particular tool—perhaps DTS when SSIS would be preferred—you can be there to suggest that they join the rest of the world in the 21st century.

A second benefit to being involved early is that as the project progresses, you will be familiar with the tasks that are associated with your name. This is important because the last thing you want to happen on the day of the production deployment is for someone to look to you to perform some task that is not even related to your job as a DBA. Believe me, it is not a pretty thing to get dragged into the whole "who does what around here" discussion. And by being involved early, you can help guide things along to make certain the right people are being called upon to perform the right functions.

TIP: Do not be frustrated if you find yourself not being involved early on in projects, just make certain you fully participate from the moment you are asked to join.

Another benefit to being involved early in any project plan is that you will be able to have clearly defined tasks to accomplish as part of the deployment. Having clearly defined tasks is a wonderful way to make certain that you can manage the expectations that others will have with regard to your role and participation. With defined tasks, you will not be concerned that someone is expecting you to "handle everything" or to "just make it work." The lines of communication should be open for all project members, making it easier to smooth out any bumps during implementation and for every member to step up to fulfill their roles and complete their tasks.

Communicate Your Actions

I have already touched upon this, but I wanted to stress this point again. *Communication is key to your success as a DBA*. Do not be afraid to tell people how long things will take. At the very least, acknowledge that you are working on a specific task. When you start a new position, you can find yourself concerned that others may not find you, say, competent. In fact, there are two likely scenarios that will pop into your mind.

You Are Not Fast Enough

Chances are you will have some apprehension about telling people how long something will take because you believe that they know how long the task should take. There is a high degree of probability that they have no idea how long something will take. What they do know, however, is how long they want something to take. If your estimate is close enough to what they want, then there is no issue. If your estimate is much longer than their current needs, then they will tell you so.

Now, if your estimate is truly the fastest amount of time it will take to perform the task, then it really won't matter one way or the other. If the estimate is not the fastest because of your experience level, then you have the following scenario.

You Did It Wrong

Let's say you tell them your estimate, you get the work done, and you provide some details on what you did. There is always a chance that they are going to respond and ask why you did something in a particular way. This may be because they have some knowledge that you do not possess, but it could also be that they are just looking for some knowledge themselves. In either case you do not need to apologize for getting a task done in a certain way. If there is a better way that you were not aware of, then admit as much and thank the person for bringing it to your attention. If there is a reason you chose to perform a specific set of actions, then feel free to explain why (politely, of course) you chose those actions, and again thank them for bringing the alternate method to your attention.

I can recall one time being questioned outright as to how and why I performed a task in a certain way. The developer was quite polite about asking me why I took a few extra steps in getting something done, and I really had no answer at the time, other than, "I preferred to do it this way and keep everything in a standard state." Another time I was ordered to perform a task in a specific way because they "wanted it done fast," and yet they were asking for it to be completed in a way that would take much longer.

It is perfectly natural to feel apprehensive about giving away too many details about the tasks you are performing. But it is my belief that you are better off communicating your actions than remaining silent. If someone suggests a different way to get something done, then you may learn something new. If someone suggests the wrong way to get something done, then you'll be presented with the opportunity to help educate someone—a win-win situation if there ever was one.

Be Responsive and Responsible

When the time comes to act, be responsive and responsible for your actions. Doing so will give others the opportunity to see you in action, to become comfortable with your skills, and to better understand that types of tasks that you are responsible for. This will in turn help you to manage their expectations over time.

Responsiveness is always going to be in the eye of the beholder. You may feel that you have done everything humanely possible to be responsive. Did you forget already that no one cares about effort? All they care about is a result, and if the result happens to be that they want you available, then that is going to be measured in terms of your responsiveness.

At the same time, however, you cannot be everything to everyone. While chances are your end users will expect you to be available 168 hours a week, the reality is that you eat, sleep, and probably also shower from time to time. This means you cannot possibly be able to respond to everything at all hours. And there are going to be times when equipment will fail, such as poor Blackberry reception, or your laptop deciding to not play nice anymore.

You will need to strike a careful balance between the two forces at play here. One the one hand will be the ever-increasing demand for your services. On the other will be your need to have a life outside of the office, which may possibly include sleep.

As funny as it may sound, being responsive is a way to help manage expectations. The more you interact with people, the more they understand what it is you do, and the more they have an idea about what they can expect from you.

Being responsible is also very important when it comes to managing expectations. You simply must be comfortable with the actions you are performing. If you make a mistake, you must admit to such. Failure to admit to a mistake can (and most often will) lead to further complications. By taking responsibility you will be demonstrating to others that you are in fact a responsible person. This will help to give them a sense that you are performing responsible actions, which is another way of saying that they will begin to develop a sense of trust.

Once you start building trust, then it is easier to manage expectations as opposed to having little to no trust. Without any trust, people will either expect you to do nothing (which is very bad) or expect you to try to do things but get them wrong (which is even worse). You can build trust by being responsible. You can be responsible for your actions, for your systems, and for your part in a project. There are many ways that you can demonstrate responsibility daily. When you see them, act upon them, start building some trust and help to manage the expectations of you as a DBA.

Time Management

You can go out and buy lots of books on time management tips and tricks. And chances are if you read enough and try enough of them, then eventually you will find something that sticks for you. But how many of those time management books were written by DBAs? Or even people that are part of IT fields in some way? While some of their tips and tricks may work, most of them may not be practical for your work as a DBA.

I have tried a *lot* of time management tricks over the course of my career. If there is one thing I have learned, it is that whatever tricks you are using today may not be effective tomorrow, and so you need to learn new ones. I once had what I thought was a wonderful habit of simply leaving whatever I was working on open so that when I came back to work the next day I could pick right up where I left off. That worked well for me until our company mandated that we reboot our desktops every night. It took me months to find a new habit that allowed for me to be as productive.

The other thing I have learned is that the most basic of techniques are the ones that stick with you the longest and are typically the most effective. These would be things like developing a routine, finding some stress relief, composing a to-do list, and working in chunks. Over time you will probably find that one technique works well for a while, then you start doing something different, and then you find yourself back with your original technique. That's fine—as long as you are doing something, it is perfectly fine to let the techniques come and go as your environment changes.

Develop a Routine

People are generally more comfortable when they have a routine to follow. I learned this cold reality most recently when my wife and I had our two children. Early on it was clear that they would function better when they had some structure to their day. We also learned that certain situations required a set of steps to be followed, and the children would often do very well following each step.

The same thing is true for your workday. Find a routine that works well for you throughout the course of the day. This helps you manage your time very well; you stay organized, you can focus on specific tasks at a time, and you'll feel a sense of accomplishment as opposed to being overwhelmed.

> **TIP:** Humans are creatures of habit; we thrive on routines. Just remember to be flexible enough in your routine to handle the unexpected that comes your way (because something unexpected will always come your way).

Having a steady routine and being able to stay in rhythm are crucial to effective time management. When you arrive at the office, you immediately know the one or two things you will review before you start your day. As your day progresses, you can continue to follow your routine and feel as if you are making progress on a task. Is every day going to be unicorns and rainbows? Of course not, but having a routine gives you a better chance at managing your time.

Part of your routine should include the review of any tasks you have automated. And speaking of automation, if you have the chance to automate something, then by all means do so. Nothing will free up your time faster than reducing your need to push a lot of buttons. If you can work into your routine some time spent on reviewing the output of automated tasks, then you will be well on your way to successful time management.

Stress Relief

Stress relief is important to time management, as it allows for you to continue operating at a higher level of efficiency. When stress hits, it will affect you in a variety of ways, one of which is your lack of focus and subsequent decrease in productivity. Not to mention the fact that you can bite someone's head off if they approach you without bearing gifts. When you start to sense that you are feeling overwhelmed and that stress is wearing you down, it is time to get up out of your cube.

Take a walk at lunch. You'll be surprised how 10 minutes around the block outside can make a big difference in your day. Go sit on a bench somewhere and watch people pass by for a few minutes. I took up jogging a few years back and find it a nice distraction during the day, especially when I have a jogging partner that I enjoy having a conversation with.

No matter what we choose to do to relieve stress, we all have one thing in common: *we select activities that energize us in some way*. That is the key to relieving stress effectively. Find something that energizes you, something you enjoy doing no matter what your mood. Of course, if you happen to find that your job is what energizes you, then you are one of the lucky ones.

Another key to relieving stress is identifying those times when you are stressed and you know to get up and do something that energizes you. This is not going to be the same for each person; you will need to find the things that work for you as well as recognize the symptoms of stress when they occur.

Now, I am often asked this question regarding stress relief and time management: "But isn't taking time away from work in fact wasting valuable work time and making it harder to get things done in the time allowed?" Absolutely not. Relieving stress will keep you productive; when you are productive, you are also efficient; when you are efficient, you are maximizing your time wisely. It really is that simple. Would you rather spend an hour dragging your heels to get through some tasks or spend 30 minutes getting some fresh air and then another 30 getting the tasks done with a clear mind?

When I was coaching basketball, I would always stress that if we prepared ourselves mentally, physically, and emotionally, then we were going to be tough to beat on any given night. Same thing for when you are at work. If you feel stress coming on and it is draining you in some way, find something to energize you, and you will be amazed at how much more productive you can become.

To-Do Lists

I started using to-do lists while in graduate school. For whatever reason, I started writing down all the things I would need to work on during the day. Big things like exams and small things like "go eat lunch." My lists would therefore be on average about a dozen items or more and typically written in the order I expected to complete them as the day went on. As I completed something, I would cross it off the list. Anything not completed would get moved to the list for tomorrow.

I did this for three years, and then stopped after leaving graduate school. I have used it on and off ever since. There are periods of my life when I feel the need to have the list in order to help me stay organized. In turn this reduces my stress levels, which we already know is important for time management. And it always makes you feel good when you get to cross something off your list.

During periods when I only have four or five things on my plate, I find it easier to go without a to-do list and simply use a routine to manage my time. Whenever I start to feel like I have taken on more than I can manage, I break out some paper and start writing things down. Once you have everything written down on a piece of paper, it really can help make all your work seem more manageable. What can seem like an overwhelming volume of work can start to seem like something you can handle with ease.

This technique does not work for everyone. My wife has tried lists and it has not been as effective as she had hoped. But the important thing here is that she tried, right? I would encourage you to do the same, as you may be surprised at how much it can help.

Chunks

Sometimes you find yourself "in the mood" to get a lot of stuff done at once. Perhaps you have a list of tasks to follow but you decide to get a little extra done for one or two of your tasks instead of moving on. Some people may start to feel that they are going to be falling behind on their list of items. Others, however, will feel great knowing that they are making more headway on one of their tasks. This is especially helpful if you have a task on your list that you know is ongoing.

While you can work on a specific chunk of a task, you can also work on little chunks of many tasks throughout your day. For some people, it will keep them engaged and energized to be working on a variety of tasks throughout the day. There are lots of days where I like to juggle a lot of items and get a little bit done on each. Then again, there are other days when I like to be very focused on one specific item.

I manage my time effectively using each of the techniques just described. Well, all of them and one more that we have not discussed yet.

Know When to Say No

Have you ever eaten at a buffet? If so, have you ever found yourself sampling a lot of different foods, only grabbing a little bit at a time—but by the time you get back to your table you have about 5 pounds of food on your plate? You know it is too much, but you feel compelled to eat everything that you took—otherwise, it would be wasteful. Well, the same thing happens when it comes to your work. You end up piling on one little thing after another, and before you know it, you have a lot more than you can handle comfortably in one sitting.

I know that I have taken on too many side projects far too often. I believe that most people can operate at peak efficiency when focusing on two things and no more. Of course, I juggle a lot more than two items each day, but it can be overwhelming when I stare at my computer screen and say, "Where do I begin?" That is when I break out the to-do list in order to make everything manageable; I can prioritize the tasks on my plate, break them into whatever size chunks I desire, build a routine, and go for a jog when I need to energize myself.

Chris Hansen and Code Reviews

Good code reviews are a necessary evil. They should be performed at regular intervals, perhaps at a project milestone or tollgate. Code reviews are a time for you to explain to your peers your thought process, as well as receive feedback on your code and design. The end result is better code, which results in a stabler system, which results in fewer production support issues. So why are most companies not bothering to do code reviews?

Because everyone dreads code reviews.

Most people are not good at presenting. To make things worse, they know they are not good and that makes them even worse. Some people could be good, but get nervous when talking in front of a group of their peers. And those that are having their code reviewed feel as if they are being interrogated by Chris Hansen from "To Catch a Predator." It all adds up to some of the most dreadful assemblies of employees you could ever hope to imagine.

So we know code reviews are important, right? And we know that everyone dreads them, and as a result no one does them anymore, right? Now, I want you to imagine that Chris Hansen is leading the code review and you are the developer currently making your presentation. You get done explaining what you are doing, and Chris starts asking you some questions, such as

CH: Do you know how old DTS is? What were you thinking? And you were not going to batch your transactions? Do you know what that will do to your log file?

You: I swear man, it was just talk, that's all it was. I wasn't going to do anything. I came here to tell my DBA that we needed to go our separate ways.

CH: Just talk? It's a lot of talk. I've got the transcript right here. You say here, "I want to cursor through all your rows." Man, that's just *wrong*.

You: I know, I know. I'm getting help. The other day I bought a book on SQL Server 2008. And I am willing to do whatever I can to help you guys. Just tell me what you want me to do.

CH: Help us?

You: Yeah, with whatever.

CH: There's the door. Go tell your friends we're watching. And the next time they hand us deployment instructions that are more complicated than a NASA launch sequence, we're coming after them.

Clearly you don't want to have things go that far, but there are going to be times when you really want to call a developer out and ask them why they have their head up their ass. Stay calm—no one person knows everything, right? But also put yourself in their shoes. If every piece of code that you just spent weeks putting together was being picked apart, you would be defensive, right? So it is natural to see the developer get defensive as well. In fact, it is natural for anyone to be somewhat defensive, even if their code is not being picked apart.

Do your best to see this as an opportunity to teach something new. Not everyone wants a lesson, however, and for those people, you need to remain calm and try your best to persuade them to see things from a different point of view. Find out their roadblock (why don't they want to do something new) and help them get around it. Over time people will begin to trust your feedback rather than think you are always on the offensive.

Chapter 5

Production Support

You are going to be responsible for supporting production systems. What you are going to find is that most people consider their system the most crucial production system. No matter what the time of day, no matter what the system, you will hear at some point, "*My* users are waiting." That translates into, "I don't care whatever else you *were* working on, fix *my* problem now so *my* users will stop complaining to me."

Yeah, it flows, and rolls, downhill. And you will have no choice but to feel you are at the bottom. No matter what else you do, you must remember to be professional in every communication you have. No flame mails, no yelling on the phone, no telling people that their system is not as important as they might think. Instead, treat each opportunity as a learning experience, see what you can take from it, and build upon it so that the next time an outage occurs, there is a reduced level of frustration for everyone.

In other words, be calm, especially if everyone else around you is starting to panic. And the best way to keep yourself calm? Make sure you have a plan, of course. And make sure you have some help.

> **TIP:** The real trick is to make everyone think that you believe their system is the most important, no matter what the circumstance.

In this chapter, we will discuss the following:

1. Why service-level agreements are important
2. How to establish a defined process for contacting support
3. How to establish a work/life balance
4. Outsourcing

ON STAYING CALM

by Jonathan Gennick

I live and work in a remote area. Services aren't what they are in the big cities. Ambulance services are part volunteer, and I'm one of the volunteers in our local service. My EMS sideline has given me some good perspective on staying calm.

First of all, nothing you face as a DBA will compare to walking into a residence during a 911 call to find your patient lying on the floor and completely unresponsive. Is it a heart attack? A low blood sugar episode? A drug reaction? Do you know what to do? Will the patient die? Will it be your fault? Once you've faced that sort of situation, you'll find that a mere database disaster just doesn't register very highly on the "it matters" meter. No one is likely to die just because the database is down, unless it's your boss from having "the big one."

Secondly, good patient care begins with staying calm. An EMS crew that gets rattled and begins to hurry too much is a crew that will make mistakes. Give me a steady and calm crew every time. Ditto in database administration. Good DBA work begins with calmness. Move slowly with deliberation. Don't rush. Take time to think.

Lastly, when confronted with something really scary, when you have that deer-in-the-headlights feeling fall over you, that's the time we in EMS fall back on our ABCs: airway, breathing, and circulation. The ABCs work for database administration, too. Can you breathe? Take a deep breath. Is air moving in and out? Put your finger on your wrist. Do you feel your pulse? If you've got those things, then relax: you've got time to think.

Service-Level Agreements

Service-level agreements (SLAs) are exactly that: agreements between two parties, often in the form of a contract, regarding a level of guaranteed service. Why do SLAs matter to you? Because you are going to be held to such an agreement. If your company is large enough to warrant a help desk or ticketing application, then chances are SLAs have been put into place already. If your company does not have those systems, then you would be wise to create your own SLAs.

Typically, such agreements will be written down. If not, then neither party will have a point of reference to work from, which will lead to confusion and frustration the next time something breaks and you are expected to fix it. You may think you have a day to resolve the matter, and the other party may think you should be done in an hour. Not good times.

SLAs can cover a wide array of topics, such as uptime, problem resolution, the amount of time to respond to a page, the number of hours you will provide coverage, and just about anything else you can imagine. Essentially, if there is a service that you are expected to provide, then having an SLA is a necessity.

I Thought We Had an Agreement?

Yeah, get used to that feeling. See, these "agreements" are subjective, and often ignored. That's especially true if everything in your environment (development, test, and production servers) is expected to be treated as production, and then on top of that everyone thinks their system is more important than anyone else's.

You may find it tempting to remind people about the SLA for their particular issue, but that will not earn you any good will. If there is a person standing in your cube, the last thing they want to hear is that you have another hour, or two, or ten before an SLA is broken. And you do not want to seem as if you are not doing anything, or deciding to do something else while there is an outage.

> **TIP:** Some people may say it is best to always look busy, and others say it is better to not be seen. I say it is best if you are not seen *and* people know you are busy.

The best advice I can give you here is to simply focus on the things that you can control, especially at that moment. Instead of reminding the customer about the true SLA time, give them an estimate on how much longer it will take for a resolution. Then, after the issue has been resolved, you should take a moment to review the defined SLAs.

I agree, and would go even further to argue that regardless of the SLA, you want to resolve an issue as quickly as possible. That is, unless you have multiple issues going on at the same time. Then you have to prioritize them based upon the SLA.

Sylvester Carstarphen

And while the use of SLAs may seem to be an imperfect system, just imagine the chaos that would exist if no SLAs were defined. Then everything would be an emergency, everyone would demand that their stuff get done quickly, and no one would ever be satisfied with whatever help you were able to provide. It can be inferred that your approval ratings are going to be directly tied to your SLA agreements, which are going to be tied to how well you manage expectations.

Get to Know What You Do

On day one you started building your initial checklist. Part of that checklist was to gather information on your databases, and to practice a few restores. That means you should have a rough idea as to how long it should take to recover some databases. This will be invaluable for those times when someone is impatiently waiting in your cube and asking, "How much longer?"

Instead of reminding them that the SLA for this particular request is the next business day, you can respond with, "The last time we did this restore it took three hours. It has only been 45 minutes, so you can expect to wait another two hours at least, if everything goes well." They still may leave your cube unhappy, but you cannot really control how they will feel. All you can control is getting the restore done, and in a timely manner.

> *Put yourself on the other end of this transaction. Say you've called the cable company to come fix a problem for you. You may not care if it takes them a couple days to do so, but you need to know that someone at the cable provider is aware of the problem and working on a solution.*
>
> Tim Gorman

If you have a help desk in place already, it may be easier for you to track your requests and make certain you are meeting your defined SLAs. If you do not have anything in place, then you should look to start grouping and classifying your requests as well as a standard resolution time. Start tracking what it is you do. Write down that you did a password reset, or that you did a restore by refreshing development from production, or that you spent time reviewing a server for any missing indexes. Get a sense for a lot of the common tasks that are coming your way and also note just how long it takes for you to resolve each of them.

> **TIP:** Document everything that you can, no matter how insignificant it may seem.

Tracking your time is going to serve you well in two ways. First, it will allow for you to give your customers realistic SLAs for a group of specific requests. Second, it helps you to better manage the expectations that will be set upon you by your customers. Think about how crucial those two items are. You will be on your way to delivering what is needed, on time, and with value.

A residual effect is that this will allow you to sit with your customers to get details on their requests. If you have demonstrated that you are able to provide quality support, then it is easier to have your customers spend an extra 5 minutes explaining some details to you that will help you to resolve their issue. That is better than the alternative, where they do not want to spend any extra time than necessary and just want you to fix something, and now.

Be Nice

When it comes to support issues, do not get caught up in flame mails. E-mail has no tone, and it is very easy to let your inner voice interpret an e-mail in a different way than was intended. If you ever think that someone is sending you a flame mail, then your best response is to pick up the phone and call them. Do not respond to them with an e-mail, as that will most likely lead to a downward spiral.

READ ME ONE MORE TIME

by Tim Gorman

When sending e-mail to customers, sometimes it is a good idea to let it sit for a few minutes while you read it over a couple times. If practical, have a trusted coworker take a look at it as well. E-mail is a great communication tool when there are details that need to be conveyed, but getting someone else's perspective on the text can be a good idea on e-mail messages that you consider important.

I've personally asked a coworker to help edit important e-mails a number of times. Following a couple of e-mail faux pas, I have become more conscious of rereading many of my e-mails before hitting the Send button.

Simply put, you must be nice. Even if someone is not being nice to you. If that is the case, then you need to find out why they are not being nice. Is it that they did not know about an SLA, did not understand the SLA, or did not care about the SLA? Could you have communicated something better? Is there a way to avoid this issue or misunderstanding in the future?

A lot of people have no idea what you do for work all day long. By the time they contact you, they are short on time. Try to keep those things in mind before you let your fingers get ahead of your brain and you click Send.

Establish Support Process

You need to clearly define how people will contact you and your team for support issues. Depending on your shop, the process could be something as simple as coming over and standing in your cube to something more complicated involving a call center application and associated work queues. If you have well-defined SLAs, then you should not have to worry about people tapping their foot in your cube waiting for a fix, right?

Well, maybe. See, even if you have a well-defined SLA, you still may have people frustrated if they do not know how to get ahold of you or your team. It is imperative that you not only define the process for contacting support, but that you publish this process so that everyone is aware.

One quick note: *do not rely on e-mail*. If you are relying on people sending e-mail as the primary means for contacting you for support, then you are setting yourself up for disappointment and frustration. Unless, of course, you expect that you are going to be able to respond to an e-mail at any time of the day or night (including weekends). I don't know about you, but every now and then I need to use the bathroom, and I typically do not offer remote support from there. I also have a tendency to sleep every now and then.

TIP: I know of one person that likes to send all e-mail alerts to the receptionist, because they are most likely to always be at or near their desk.

Define Process

You need to have a clear, easy-to-follow process for production support defined. It should be as streamlined as possible, with very few handoffs between people or systems. When someone wants to contact you, they should be able to do so in a simple manner. I like to define any process with the thought that I am *not* immediately available. For example, I could be driving through a tunnel and not have good reception for my phone.

The start of your process would begin with someone needing to contact you, so think about how you want that contact to happen. You have three choices: they can call you on the phone, they can send you an e-mail, or they can walk over to your cube. As I said before, try to build your process with the assumption that you will not be immediately available. Therefore, telling people to stop by your cubicle would not be the best possible choice. Same for e-mail, as there is a chance that you will not always have your eyes glued to your inbox. The choice that allows for the highest probability of success is a telephone call.

Sure, you could miss a phone call, no question. But when you think about the number of e-mails you get a day vs. the number of phone calls, you can see that phone calls stand out as something *different*, and you are going to pay more attention to your phone ringing than to an e-mail.

If we were to assume that someone calls and leaves a message, how long would you have to respond? The answer, of course, is that you have as long as your SLA defines. And that means it depends upon the nature of the emergency. Which means you need to have a process in place that satisfies the highest possible SLA-defined response time, and chances are an e-mail at 3 a.m. is not going to suffice.

> **TIP:** I'm not sure about you, but I enjoy sleeping. Keep in mind that others enjoy that as well when you start building out your systems and defined SLAs.

If you are fortunate enough to be able to hire an answering service, I would recommend doing so. This way you can rest assured that someone will always be available to answer the phone and that they will in turn make an attempt to contact you or your team immediately afterward. Whether or not you have the luxury of an answering service, you should make certain that there is only one phone number used as the primary contact number.

An example of a process using many of the above details would look as follows:

1. The customer calls a production support number.
2. The call is answered by answering service.
3. The message is taken, including customer information details.
4. The answering service calls the specified phone number.
5. The call is answered by the DBA responsible for support.

That is a very simple version of a defined support process, but there is a lot of work that goes into making this happen. Working backward, how do you make certain that the answering service contacts the correct DBA? One way is to rotate a pager, but you may be fortunate enough to have people assigned to support specific applications or sites.

Going further backward, how do you make certain that the customer calls the correct number for DBA production support? Let's look at the answer to that question next.

Publish Process

You need to publish your defined production support process. It must be communicated clearly, and it will need to be communicated often. And no matter how many times you communicate the process to your customers, there is always going to be someone that tells you they had no idea about the process. Remember, *be nice*.

Look for creative ways to advertise the support process. Instead of sending out company-wide e-mails detailing the process, you could be subtler and simply include the correct phone numbers in your e-mail signature. You could also publish the process to an internal web site and refer people to that link when appropriate. Still another option would be to publish reports on the volume of support calls you handle per month and include the process details inside the report (as opposed to just reporting on the numbers and assuming everyone knows the process).

> **TIP:** You could publish this info ten times over and people will still miss things or deny having read them. Be patient when they claim ignorance, and simply forward them the materials again.

You will need to publish wherever you can, remind people periodically (somehow), and make certain people are notified about the process, especially if and when changes are made.

Remind and Enforce

You will constantly need to remind people about your production support process. Most people are not going to pay attention to any process that they do not use on a regular basis. And if things are going well in your shop, then people will not need to be contacting you for help, which means they will most likely not be as familiar with the process as they should be.

Besides reminding people about the process, you will also need to enforce the process. This is where it pays to be nice. If someone contacts you for production support and does not follow the defined process, you have two choices. You can assist them and remind them of the process, or you can remind them of the process and make them follow it before you assist them.

While you may think that the right choice is to help the person and then remind them about the correct process, stop and think about that scenario for a moment. If they did not need to follow the process and you helped them anyway, why would they change their ways the next time around? Remember that if things are going well in your shop, then most people will not need to contact you on a regular basis. So, when exactly would they start to become familiar with the process?

As painful as it may be to do so, and even at the risk of your approval ratings, sometimes it is best to remind people about the correct process. Usually I try to weigh the situation at hand to decide if I am going to enforce the process or if I am going to allow the person to bypass the process altogether. No matter which one I choose, I do my best be nice.

Work/Life Balance

When you are designing your production support process, it is important to remember that you have a life outside of work. Failure to recognize this fact could result in your designing a process that isn't sustainable over a long period of time. Even if you don't think you have a life, do your best to assume that you do; otherwise, your design process will be built around the assumption that you are always available. That means you have a single point of failure, which is going to result in poor service to someone at some point in time.

One aspect that tends to get overlooked is the ability to know when to say no. In today's corporate culture, many people feel that they are not allowed to say no when asked to take on extra assignments. If you say no too often, then soon enough people will stop asking, and it will not be long before your services will no longer be required altogether.

It is important to have some downtime away from your work responsibilities. This allows you to recharge your batteries, so to speak. You can reduce your stress level and get some needed rest, and when you return to work find yourself refreshed. But if work is so demanding that you are constantly needed at all hours, how do you balance your work life and your home life?

Communication

Like most things in life, good communication is critical to making everything run smoothly. This is no exception. Good communication between you, your manager, and your family is essential when trying to balance your work and your personal time.

If you need to work late or on the weekend, then notify your family as soon as you are aware. Will you be able to do so in a timely enough manner for their liking? No, not always. But at least you are making the attempt. I find it useful to share a calendar with my family so that I am always aware of everyone's activities at home when I know my work responsibilities will infringe upon family time.

> **TIP:** Know when to say no, but always say yes to your family. Always.

If your family needs you, then communicate that to your manager as soon as you are aware. If you need to leave early, say your child is sick and tell your manager. Most companies these days offer what is commonly called flex time; there is no clock to punch, so if you need to leave early infrequently, then you can do so, providing that you make up for the time later on.

I know that a lot of people are going to tell you that you family must come before your work. I will not disagree with that, but would add that you need to be mindful of your duties and obligations to each.

Protect Your Private Time

When you are home and not on call or expected to respond to anyone at work, then put the Blackberry in a different room. Believe me, the world will not end if you do not read or respond to an e-mail until the morning. If something is important, then someone should be calling your Blackberry, not sending you an e-mail, so just make certain you can hear your phone ring.

Your job performance should be tied to tangible results, not the amount of hours that you put in working. If the number of hours seems to be all that matters, then you will find yourself with less personal time, and the company will more than likely find itself with less-than-ideal results from your performance. It is OK to let people know that when you are home, you are home. Many people believe that by protecting their home life, they end up enhancing the quality of the work they produce during regular working hours.

Happy Fun Play Time

You need to keep your stress level low, and one way to do that is to stay involved with activities you find fun and enjoyable. Have a hobby? Set aside some time weekly to pursue that hobby. Find those things that are important to you; things that are important enough for you to set aside some time. You are the one that controls your schedule, so use that to your advantage.

What I look for are things that energize me. It can be anything—writing, tuning queries, jogging—whatever. The point is that I know there are certain activities that engage me at different times of the day and week, and those activities energize me as opposed to draining me physically, mentally, and emotionally.

You are not always going to have equal amounts of time for work and life activities. But what you *can* do is only find time for work and life activities that you find energizing. Work and life are fluid events—some days you need to do more of one than the other, much to your dismay usually. But if those activities are *giving* you energy, then you are less likely to suffer from burnout.

Your schedule should reflect this; give yourself some wiggle room each day to allow for your work or life to run longer than expected. That way, you never feel like you are leaving something out. What's more is that as you finish up a task for either one, you will finish it feeling energized, not drained. You should feel like you accomplished something and be looking forward to the next task.

THE "TODAY" LIST

by Jonathan Gennick

I begin each workday by creating a to-do list specifically for that day. Years ago, I would try to cram as many items on the list as I thought I could fit. Don't do that. It's a trap. As Tom points out, workdays never go purely as planned, and you need to leave some margin for error. I still create a daily list, but I leave a generous margin to handle all the ad hoc items that hit me as the day progresses. The to-do list gives me a target that—if I can hit it—lets me go home feeling proud of having given a good effort and accomplishing some tangible results.

Outsourcing

The term *outsourcing* has a negative connotation associated with it these days. In fact, most times I ask people to share their experiences with outsourcing, their responses are more negative than positive. The reasons vary, but I have grouped them into the following categories:

- Poor quality of work
- Language barriers
- Security
- Fear of losing one's job

Years ago, as I was becoming overwhelmed with the growing volume of work, my manager told me that the only alternative we had at the time was to outsource some of my workload. I was tentative for a handful of reasons, some of which I just noted. But my apprehension was not enough to stop me from trying, as I knew that the mountain of work was not going to be done without some help.

I had a choice: I could fail miserably at trying to manage my workload, or I could give outsourcing a chance; if it failed, at least I would have tried to do something. As I look back upon the decision to outsource a large bulk of our workload, I realize that it was probably one of the best decisions of my career.

Before we decided to dive into hiring anyone, my manager and I went over all of our concerns. We listed them out and then did our best to come up with ideas to mitigate them. After all, failure to plan is planning to fail, right? We had never set out to fail before, and decided that we didn't want to fail on something as important as this.

How did we manage to have success? Well, let's look at each of the groups I listed and help to mitigate some of your fears.

Quality of Work

At the top of many people's list when it comes to outsourcing is the concern that the quality of work will be poor. And for many this is no doubt true. But we decided to examine why there is a perception of poor quality. We asked around to find other companies that were using outsourcing, in the attempt to find out what was and wasn't working for each particular company.

What we found was that tasks that could be identified as *operational* were usually considered to be done with a high rate of quality. Tasks that were defined as *nonoperational* were usually considered to have poor quality. Believe me, it was that simple. All it took was asking around, talking to some peers, finding out what was and wasn't working, and putting them into two groups.

As a DBA, we have many tasks that are considered operational in nature. To me, an operational task is something that can be followed through repetition—it rarely changes, and the outcome is typically known. Consider database backups. Configuring backups—making certain they complete successfully—is an operational task. So is a database restore. As are password resets, production change deployments, data migrations, and even some basic troubleshooting.

> **TIP:** If you have documented things well, then it should be very easy to determine if quality is suffering as a result of outsourcing.

The first step is to document exactly how such tasks are done in your shop. Once you have that document, you then hand it off to your outsource team and give them a chance to provide the same level of support. Either they can, which is great, or they cannot, and you move along to find someone else.

And if the worst thing to come from all of this is that you finally spend the time to document some of your daily tasks, then you will be in better shape anyway. After all, you know you are already sinking under a mountain of work and that you need help from someone. Having your procedures written down is a necessity in order to make certain that any new hire can be brought up to speed in the shortest time.

Whenever we noticed that our offshore team could not provide the level of support necessary for our customers, we did not react by saying, "We need to find someone better." Our first reaction was, "How can we make the process simpler and improve our documentation?"

In time, we were able to streamline our processes and improve our documentation, and our offshore team was able to provide the support necessary for all the tasks we could classify as operational.

Language Barriers

It is a life goal of mine to live and work in the south of France. Anywhere would be fine, really—I am not picky. A quick search for technical jobs in France shows more than a handful that I am qualified for. So, why am I not living and working in France right now?

Because I don't speak the language well enough to work as a database professional. And speaking the native language is a fairly important skill to have.

Are there any database professional jobs available for someone that has limited language skills? Probably, but how much time do I want to spend trying to arrange for interviews with people I do not know? It would be better for me to let my network know I am interested and then wait for the right opportunity to find me.

> **TIP:** I always admire people that take the time to learn a second language, and I do my best to help them communicate when possible.

Let's reverse the scenario and suppose that someone from another country comes to me looking for a job. Would I hire them if they had all the necessary skills except being able to communicate in English? Of course not—no one would hire someone that cannot speak the language for a job that requires good communication skills.

> *I also like to evaluate the importance of the candidate's communication skills when interviewing them. If you are going to be required to communicate with customers, then the ability to speak clearly is important. If you only interact with the DBA team, I may be more forgiving when it comes to your ability to speak clearly.*
>
> Sylvester Carstarphen

And yet that is a common practice with outsourcing. For whatever reason, people simply accept someone with below-average communication skills instead of saying, "I'm sorry, but we need someone that can speak our language better." We never hesitated when it came to communication skills. If I was not able to understand a candidate during the interview, then my customers would have no chance of understanding them.

So we held out for a candidate that could communicate, and emphasized that over technical skills. I felt I could teach anyone the skills they needed, but I could not teach them English. I did not need a senior administrator; I would take a junior administrator that could speak well instead. And in order to handle any turnover, we would always keep a shadow resource on staff so that we could easily transition new members to the team without suffering loss of support.

Security

Another common concern with outsourcing centers on the security of the company's data. I am certain that this is a natural concern and a valid one in today's global electronic society, but I also never understood how it is different than when you hire any new employee. I suppose you may say that it is different because the outsource team is outside your network, or that you cannot see what they are doing while at their desks, but there are plenty of ways to monitor their activities if necessary. Besides, the risk of data theft is real enough and can happen from anywhere—inside your network as well as outside.

We listed this as a concern as well when we first started. So much so that we talked about not allowing our outsource team to handle anything related to security. After a while, we understood that many security requests are operational in nature, and we made an easy transition to have those tasks outsourced. After all, we needed them to perform these tasks so that we could free up time to focus on some larger issues with regard to instance configurations, baselines, and monitoring.

I would suggest that you treat your outsource partner as you would any other partner when it comes to matters of security. Define what tasks are allowable; you may have some security items that are not allowed to be done by anyone else. And keep in mind that there is a difference between what you *need* to remain in house and what you *want* to remain.

Job Security

One summer during college I had a job doing piece work in a furniture factory. Essentially, I would assemble different pieces of what would become frames for things like chairs and sofas. I rarely ever saw the finished product, as all we were contracted to do was build a frame and send it off to a different shop where they would finish the actual piece.

As I started getting used to the environment and the work, I also started getting faster at producing my pieces. I would get started, figure out an efficient way to maximize my output, and focus on getting the job done. I enjoyed the work and enjoyed keeping track of how well I was doing. The man working next to my table would keep pace with me as well. We could talk while we worked and managed to get a lot of work done.

> **TIP:** You should spend more time focusing on your own efforts and less time worrying about someone else. Focus on what you can control; otherwise, you will quickly become frustrated.

One day we were approached by a coworker who said simply, "Slow down; you guys are making us look bad."

I had no idea that my doing good work would be considered a bad thing by others. Sure, I was aware of things like how a person doing well on an exam can throw off the grading curve for the whole class, but this was different. First, this man was serious.

Second, he had access to lots of tools and machines that could hurt me, especially in an industrial "accident." I didn't know what to say, but the man next to me sure did: "Get out of here," he said. "Try doing some work yourself for a change, and don't ever tell us we are going too fast. The only one making you look bad is yourself."

When it comes to outsourcing, many people are apprehensive. They do not want to see the tasks they perform being done by someone else, and they especially don't want someone else to start doing them better than they were able to do. This is a natural reaction and quite understandable. Except, well, I don't understand it.

Maybe it is the Tom Sawyer in me, but if I can find someone else to paint the fence for me, I will. I have never felt threatened by letting someone else take on tasks that I was doing. I always saw that as an opportunity for me to start doing something new and greater. I would be allowed to shift my focus, learn new things, take on greater responsibilities, and grow as an individual.

I was never afraid of handing tasks to our outsource team. I would have people in our department tell me, "If you give them too much work, then there won't be any need to keep you." I could never understand that way of thinking. From the moment we decided to outsource, I was only looking forward and never worried about losing my own job.

All Good Things

My outsourcing experience has been quite positive. Apparently I am an aberration, according to the many people who talk about how bad it is to outsource. What I find funny is when someone considers outsourcing to mean that a particular role or function is sent overseas, and doesn't understand that hiring a contractor to come onsite is the same thing. If you are hiring someone to help you with some defined tasks, does it really matter where they sit? Why are you comfortable if they sit next to you and do part of your job, and not as comfortable if they are not near you?

One of the biggest benefits that outsourcing has for me is to make me focus on defining our current processes—very helpful when someone demands to see that you have something documented even though they (1) don't really care and (2) don't understand it anyway. Having your stuff documented is necessary anyway. Plus, if your support breaks down, you can go back to your documents and make certain they are clear enough for everyone to understand. If they are, then it allows you to review the process and try making it simpler. In the end, you'll have a stabler environment, and one that is easier to maintain. And one that allows for you to keep your customers happy. Trust me, they like to be happy.

Chapter 6

Basic Troubleshooting

Your phone is going to ring, and the voice on the other end is going to say something incredibly descriptive such as "the server is slow," or "is the server OK right now," or one of my favorites, "we had a problem last night at 3AM, did you see anything wrong at that time?"

When the time comes to drill down to the root cause of performance issues you are going to want to quickly isolate the nature of the issue. Knowing what tools you have at your disposal is only part of the solution; the other part is knowing how to apply the right tools, and at the right time.

This chapter will give you a solid foundation on basic troubleshooting techniques and tools. You will need to be able to troubleshoot issues if you want to survive as a DBA. Performance tuning skills will come later. Right now, you need to be able to isolate the problems if you expect to come back to work each Monday.

> **TIP:** I would estimate that roughly seventy percent of all performance issues I have seen are the result of code, and not the database engine. Code can be stored procedures, queries, database design or schema, or indexes. Sometimes it is simply the result of an influx of data. Keep all that in mind when troubleshooting any performance issue.

In this chapter, we will discuss the following:

1. CSI: SQL
2. Common Bottlenecks
3. Available Tools

CSI: SQL

Think of the job of a police detective assigned to the forensics unit. No matter what time of day or night, when a crime happens they will be called to investigate. They make certain the scene is secure, they gather their evidence, interview witnesses and suspects, and do their best to solve the crime. Not only will they need to interview people but they will need to set up surveillance on their suspects and monitor their activities for a period of time.

On television all of this happens in less than an hour. In real life, it takes a little bit longer. And some crimes never get solved.

Now think about your life as a DBA. No matter what time of the day or night someone, somewhere, is going to have an issue with a database or a database server. When that happens, you are going to get called in to investigate. You will be expected to immediately analyze all available details and provide a recommended course of action. If your job was a television show, you would be given about an hour to solve the issue. In real life, people want an answer in less than a few minutes, especially if it is the middle of the night. And rarely are your issues allowed to go unsolved.

In order to provide high level of support you will need to make certain you can do three things. First, you need to know where to look, which we will assume to mean an incident has taken place. Second, you need to know what questions to ask (and who to ask), which you can think of as an interview (or an interrogation). And third, either review your monitoring or put your monitoring in place, which is the same as surveillance.

That is the DBA circle of life: something will happen, you will ask some questions, and you need to monitor some things going forward.

Incidents

Incidents and issues will happen; there is no way to avoid them. All you can really do is make certain you are as prepared as possible to deal with them when they happen. You can best achieve this by approaching each issue in the same exact way, much as a forensics detective would. In addition to having your own set of tools at your disposal, another good skill to acquire is the ability to *remain unemotional*.

If you allow emotions to be a factor in your work then you will likely have clouded judgment. You need to focus on the facts at hand. Allowing your emotions to come into play can cause you to overlook facts or clues that are right in front of you. This can lead you to make a poor recommendation on a course of action.

> **TIP:** Do not lay blame for the incident on someone that was not involved in any way. Gather your facts so that you can arrive at sound conclusions.

When an incident arises you need to get involved and gather all the facts you can and then analyze those facts. Chances are you will feel pressure to solve the issue; do not let that pressure dictate your actions.

Always check your work. If you think you know the answer after only a few minutes of investigation then go back and check again to see if there is anything you may have missed.

Only after you have gathered your facts will you be ready to start asking some pertinent questions.

Interrogations

The facts that you gather will lead you to questions that need to be answered.

Let's consider the following scenario. It is the middle of the night. A scheduled process has filled up the data drive on the server. You get called in to investigate, you gather your facts, and you can see the exact database that is responsible for the unexpected growth. You could dive in and start trying to solve the issue but the right thing to do is to start asking questions.

Is the space needed? Was this growth expected, but not properly planned for? Is there some cleanup that can be done? Can the drive be expanded? If so, how long will it take?

If you are lucky, the people that can answer your questions will be immediately available. That is not always going to be the case. When asking questions you will need to make certain you do so in a way that does not make them feel as if it is a police interrogation. You will need to have good soft skills (and patience) in order to draw out all the necessary details.

One way to get this done is by focusing on the process. Let the people know that you are trying to help and that in order to get them the help they need then there is a process to be followed. Part of the process is to ask questions in order to make certain all relevant facts are known. If you fail to make that connection then people will tend to react to you as if they are being questioned by the police.

However, there are going to be times when you do everything in your power to make people feel as if they are part of the process, but they still choose to not participate. You cannot force people to talk; either they want to work with you on a proper solution or not. Even if you know they have the details you need, if they choose to remain silent, or choose to work by themselves, all you can do is work with the facts and answers you have. You are not allowed to sit them in a cold room with bright lights for hours on end, no matter how much you think they deserve such treatment.

Of course, one reason people may not want to answer your questions is because they don't want to incriminate themselves. If you have your surveillance in place then your questions can be focused, but remember to remain emotionally detached.

Surveillance

Most senior DBA's have some level of proactive monitoring in place. This allows for them to see changes in the environment, which helps them know where to look and what questions to ask when issues arise. But how do they know what to monitor in the first place?

Everyone starts with some basic monitoring of their environment, but over time you may find yourself monitoring some oddball items. This is often the result of a previous incident followed by a knee-jerk reaction in which you are asked (or ordered) to start monitoring something in particular.

> **NOTE:** I'm reminded of the airline security practice of removing shoes. That practice is a classic example of a single incident leading to the type of reaction-oriented monitoring that Tom talks about. Some of what you monitor will be a similar result of your employer's or client's specific history. — Jonathan Gennick.

For example, many companies monitor their database backups to ensure that they have run successfully. But not many have a process in place to verify if the database backups can be restored in a timely fashion. All it takes is one time where you are not able to complete a restore and you will find yourself being asked to monitor your database backups more closely. In one particular case, this meant I needed to develop a process that would verify the database backups were still available on disk, because waiting a day to recover from tape was not considered acceptable.

Another item to consider is that your monitoring solution needs to mitigate the incidents that are occurring. If something happens once and you are not able to provide an answer immediately, you may buy some time by explaining how you will put some better monitoring into place. But if the same incidents continue to happen and you are no closer to a solution despite your efforts to monitor the situation, then you had better believe that people's confidence in your abilities will wane.

As time goes by, you will find that your monitoring solution will develop as a reaction to incidents and issues that have arisen. What really matters is the end result, which is that you need to have tools in place to recreate events or to watch events as they unfold.

Common Bottlenecks

Issues with SQL Server are usually grouped into three main categories: disk I/O, memory, or CPU. As such, those three items are good places to begin when trying to troubleshoot any particular issue. When the phone rings in the middle of the night you want to start ruling out as many suspects as possible. Doing so will allow for you to focus on finding the true root cause of the issue.

Most likely, all you will ever be told is that the server is "slow." The end user has little to no idea as to the nature of the problem; they just want their problem to disappear. It is up to you to know where, and how, to analyze the situation. Therefore, you should become familiar with the most common bottlenecks and how to quickly diagnose if any one of them is the issue. Later in this chapter in the section "Available Tools," I will discuss some of the various tools you have at your disposal right out of the box. I will explain how each tool can be used to find out more about disk I/O, memory, and CPU. In the next sections, I will explain how and why each is important and what role they play in your overall performance.

Disk

If you are using a database then you have the need for data to be written to and read from disks. You want your data to be written to disk as fast as possible. You want your data read from disks just as quickly. You also want your disks to have adequate space to store all of your data. All of this requires adequate planning as well as some performance tuning. Unfortunately, in the middle of the night you will not have the luxury of doing one or the other. You will need to have a method for quickly determining if disk I/O is an issue, either as a root cause or a symptom of something else.

Unless your database is of a small enough size to fit entirely inside of the server's memory, your performance is going to be dependent upon your disk I/O. This is because the database engine will be constantly swapping data pages from memory to disk and vice versa. SQL Server will also use tempdb to store data and the transaction log will need to flush pages to disk as well.

That is a lot of I/O activity for one database. Data, logs, and tempdb all need to read and write data from disk. Now consider that you probably have more than just one database on your server. It is easy to see how disk I/O can be a bottleneck for any server. Proper alignment of data files, log files, and tempdb is essential for good performance.

Memory

Applications need to use computer memory in order to run, and SQL Server is no exception. You may find yourself having memory pressure that is either physical or virtual in nature, and in both cases the pressure may be internal or external. Before you dive into such details, you need to be able to determine if memory pressure even exists. Just because SQL Server is consuming memory does not mean that there is a problem.

I like to set the memory for my database servers to be the same fixed size for both the maximum and minimum memory configurations. On a dedicated database server, I will leave just enough memory for the base operating system to function, typically 2–3GB, and assign the rest to SQL Server. This can result in a situation where your phone will ring and the voice on the other end will say "SQL is consuming a lot of memory, please do something to fix the situation." Of course there is nothing for you to fix, because you have configured it to operate that way!

If the SQL service is indeed operating at or near capacity then you may start to see error messages that pertain to memory. If you recall, I already talked about how SQL will swap data pages between memory and disk. The area of memory used is called the *buffer pool*. Reading from memory is faster than reading from disk, so the more you can store in the buffer pool the faster your performance will be.

But when your server is under memory pressure, your buffer pool will not be able to handle the increase in requests, and performance will degrade. That's when your phone will ring.

CPU

CPU spikes will happen from time to time and are typically defined by having the available CPUs more than 80 percent utilized. CPU spikes represent a dichotomy; you don't want to see your CPU's being over utilized and yet you also want to use your available CPU's otherwise they are sitting there idle. Allowing a resource to sit idle could be considered to be a waste, right? So, you have to make certain your CPU's are being used efficiently, but not taxed to the point that the server itself is overburdened.

CPU spikes are typically the result of query plans that have changed for the worse. But they could also be the result of something else, perhaps your hardware is no longer sufficient or maybe a recent configuration change has caused your CPU to spike. You will typically be asked to investigate a CPU spike *after* the issue has started, and not before. Therefore, you will need to find ways to find the specific activity that is causing the CPU to spike. You will examine some of those ways in the next section.

Another thing to keep in mind is that query plans can change for a variety of reasons. One of the main reasons for a change in plans is a result of a change in the underlying data. All too often I have seen issues with CPU performance as a result of a bad plan caused by data inserts, updates, and deletes. The hard part is knowing whether a plan has gone bad or not. The only way to know if it has gone bad (other than the CPU spike) is to have an idea of what the original (or good) plan looked like.

If you do not have a copy of the good plan, then it would not be a correct assumption to simply state that your query plans have gone bad. Even if you look at the plan and see nothing but table scans and hash matches you still cannot assert that the plan has "gone bad," unless you have something to compare it with. Therefore, keep that in mind before you rush to make any judgments. Focus on the facts, do your best to isolate the queries that are consuming the most CPU, and then go from there.

Available Tools

SQL Server ships with a variety of tools available for you to quickly diagnose and troubleshoot performance issues. In addition to those tools, the Windows OS also has some tools that will be of use to you when trying to track down the root cause of performance problems. Below I have listed some of the tools you will have at your disposal. I have also tried to break them all down in such a way to help you understand how each one can be used to troubleshoot issues related to disk I/O, memory, and CPU.

Reliability and Performance Monitor

Windows Server 2008 introduces the Reliability and Performance Monitor. This is the latest version of what was previously called Performance monitor (or perfmon for short). In fact, if you were to run the command perfmon from a Win2008 server it will launch the new version.

Figure 6–1 shows the Resource Overview immediately after running the perfmon command. You can click on any one of the graphs displayed and it will expand the corresponding menu located below. In the upper left of the window, you will see that there are two options listed under Monitoring Tools. One is the Performance Monitor, which will be familiar to anyone that has used perfmon in the past. The other is the newer Reliability Monitor, which you can use to examine details about the stability of the server.

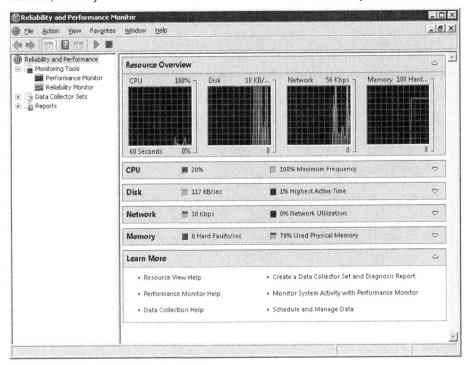

Figure 6–1. *The new Reliability and Performance Monitor*

The Resource Overview will allow for you to quickly drill into details regarding disk I/O, memory, and CPU usage. If you want to go into more detail or if you are using previous versions of Windows server, then you will want to use Performance Monitor to gather information on the current server activity. When clicking on the Performance Monitor name in the upper-left corner you will see something similar to Figure 6–2.

Note that in Win2008 the only counter selected is the % Processor Time. In previous versions of Performance Monitor, more than one counter will be selected by default (Avg. Disk Queue Length and Pages/Sec). After navigating to this screen, you are going to need to add new counters in order to get the details for each potential bottleneck.

If you want additional details on any of the counters I mention below, you can either refer to the Books On-Line entries or go to http://msdn.microsoft.com/en-us/library/ms191246(SQL.90).aspx for more information on what values are considered to be good, bad, or indifferent.

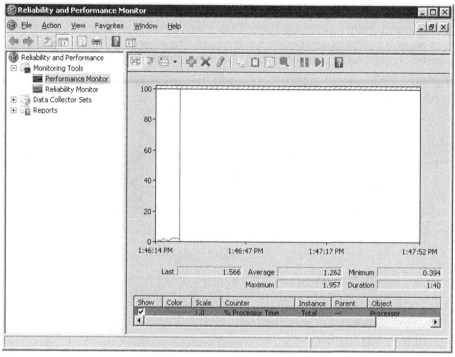

Figure 6–2. *CPU utilization in the Performance Monitor*

Disk I/O

I mentioned earlier how SQL will swap data from disk to memory and vice versa, and how there is a lot of I/O activity on your database server with data files, log files, and tempdb activity all happening at the same time. While SQL manages how the activities occur, it is Windows OS that actually does the work, and that is why using performance counters is a good way to understand exactly what is happening on your server.

SQLServer:PhysicalDisk

The two objects that are most useful are the SQLServer:PhysicalDisk and the SQLServer:Buffer Manager. Following are the physical disc counters to watch:

- % Disk Time
- Avg. Disk Queue Length
- Avg. Disk sec/Read
- Avg. Disk sec/Write
- Avg. Disk Reads/sec
- Avg. Disk Writes/sec

One thing to note here is that your queue length should not be greater than one or two on average *per disk*. So, if you have a RAID striped set of seven disks and you see an average disk queue length of eight, you are still well within an acceptable working range.

SQLServer:Buffer Manager

There are two buffer manager counters to watch. They are as follows:

- Page Reads/sec
- Page Writes/sec

Memory

There are a handful of counters available for you to examine with regard to memory pressure. If you recall I talked about how SQL uses a buffer cache in order to store data pages in memory before swapping the data out to disk. Therefore, it should not be a surprise to find that some of the counters you want to examine are located in the SQLServer:Buffer Manager object and are as follows:

- Buffer cache hit ratio
- Page life expectancy
- Checkpoint pages/sec
- Lazy writes/sec
- Total Pages

Something that warrants mentioning: memory pressure and I/O bottlenecks are typically related, due to the nature of how SQL swaps data to and from disk and into memory.

Additional counters related to memory can be found inside the SQLServer:Memory manager object. They are as follows:

- Available Bytes
- Pages/sec
- Total Server Memory (KB)

CPU

I mentioned how query plans that have gone bad can cause CPU spikes. Recompilations are another way for your CPU to have a sudden surge in usage. The counters you will want to add are found in the **SQLServer:SQL Statistics object** and are as follows:

- Batch Requests/sec
- SQL Compilations/sec
- SQL Recompilations/sec

The number of recompilations should be low, and the ratio of recompilations to actual batch requests should be very low. If these are high then you may see a CPU spike, or you could have a high frequency of ad-hoc queries.

Another possible cause of CPU spikes is the usage of cursors. Well, to be more precise, the poor usage of cursors. Cursors themselves are not necessarily a bad thing, but when not properly designed and cared for they can lead to performance problems that are manifested by CPU spikes. The counter you want to examine for this case is found in the SQLServer:Cursor Manager by Type: Cursor Requests/sec.

Activity Monitor

The Activity Monitor in SQL Server 2008 Management Studio (SSMS) has undergone a facelift from the 2005 version. For starters, you access the Activity Monitor by right-clicking on the instance name inside of SSMS and select "Activity Monitor." The monitor displays four graphs and four rows to help you understand more details regarding the processes that are currently being run by the database engine. See Figure 6–3 for an example.

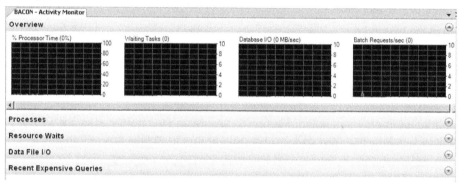

Figure 6–3. *SQL Server 2008 Management Studio's Activity Monitor*

The information being displayed is taken from Dynamic Management Views being run against the instance. That means the information you see displayed is real time. However, it only goes as far back as the last time the instance was started.

Disk I/O

The Data File I/O section will return information on the data and log files for the system and user databases. You can sort and filter on columns for MB/sec Read, MB/sec Written, and Response Time. This is a very quick and easy way to see if there is disk I/O contention for any particular data or log file.

Memory

The only part of the Activity Monitor that pertains to memory is found in the Processes section which has a column named Memory Use (KB). This column simply shows the amount of memory that is being used by a particular query. If you are having memory issues, then chances are you will not be able to use this section to isolate one particular query, as it could be the sum total of all the queries currently running.

CPU

There are two places inside of Activity Monitor to find pertinent information on CPU usage. One is inside of the Resource Waits section, where there is a wait category appropriately named CPU. You can then use that information to filter the queries in the Processes tab to isolate the processes that are currently waiting for CPU.

The other section to find information on CPU usage is in the Recent Expensive Queries. There you will see roughly ten to fifteen recent queries and you can sort by the CPU (ms/sec) column. This is especially handy because you will most likely be called to investigate after an issue has happened, so being able to review the recent queries that have been run against the instance is valuable information to review.

Dynamic Management Views (DMVs)

SQL 2005 introduced the use of Dynamic Management Views and functions. These are views that will return information about your server instance and databases and are useful for diagnosing performance issues. You access the views and functions with T-SQL only, as if you were querying from a table. All of the DMV's are located inside the sys schema. If you want to browse them inside of SSMS then you will need to navigate to the system views inside of individual databases, as shown in Figure 6–4.

The information returned by querying a DMV is reset when the instance is restarted. So any information returned is only going to give you a look at the system since that last restart. This means you cannot use a DMV for historical purposes, unless you are gathering and storing the data in a repository manually yourself. Of course, if you are having performance issues now, then DMV's are going to be giving you a real-time look at what is happening, and that can be valuable information to aid in your analysis.

If you want specific details about DMV's you can find them at: http://msdn.microsoft.com/en-us/library/ms188754.aspx. The following list shows some of the DMV's I believe you will find most useful for basic troubleshooting, but will not go into much detail. I would encourage you to do some independent research about DMV's as the best way to learn about them and what they can do for you is to start experiencing them for yourself.

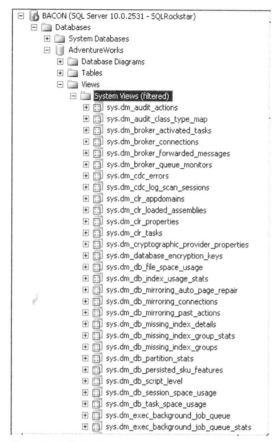

Figure 6–4. *Navigating to the dynamic management views*

Disk I/O

Some of the DMV's that will help you to determine disk I/O issues include the following:

- sys.dm_db_file_space_usage
- sys.dm_db_index_operational_stats
- sys.dm_db_index_usage_stats
- sys.dm_exec_query_stats
- sys.dm_exec_query_plan
- sys.dm_io_virtual_file_stats
- sys.dm_io_pending_io_requests
- sys.dm_os_wait_stats
- sys.dm_os_waiting_tasks

Here is an example T-SQL script that will help you use the sys.dm_io_virtual_file_stats DMV to find data files that are producing the highest average number of milliseconds per I/O:

```
SELECT io_stall / (num_of_reads + num_of_writes) AS avg_ms_per_io,
    io_stall AS io_stall_ms,
    (num_of_reads + num_of_writes) AS num_io,
    DB_NAME (database_id) AS database_name,
    file_id
FROM sys.dm_io_virtual_file_stats (null, null)
WHERE (num_of_reads + num_of_writes) > 500
ORDER BY 1 DESC
```

Memory

Some of the DMV's that will help you to determine memory issues include the following:

- sys.dm_os_cache_counters

- sys.dm_os_memory_clerks

- sys.dm_os_memory_cache_clock_hands

- sys.dm_os_process_memory

- sys.dm_os_ring_buffers

- sys.dm_os_sys_memory

- sys.dm_os_virtual_address_dump

- sys.dm_os_wait_stats

- sys.dm_os_waiting_tasks

Here is an example T-SQL script that will help you use the sys.dm_os_buffer_descriptors DMV to find the databases that have the most data pages currently residing in the buffer pool:

```
SELECT COUNT(*) AS cached_pages,
        CASE database_id WHEN 32767 THEN 'ResourceDb'
                ELSE DB_NAME(database_id)
        END AS [database]
FROM sys.dm_os_buffer_descriptors
GROUP BY DB_NAME(database_id), database_id
ORDER BY cached_pages DESC
```

CPU

Some of the DMV's that will help you to determine CPU issues include the following:

- sys.dm_exec_cached_plans

- sys.dm_exec_query_stats

- sys.dm_exec_query_optimizer_info

- sys.dm_exec_requests

- sys.dm_exec_sessions

- sys.dm_os_schedulers

- sys.dm_os_wait_stats

- sys.dm_os_waiting_tasks

Here is an example T-SQL script that will help you use the sys.dm_os_schedulers DMV to locate possible CPU issues by identifying the number of tasks currently waiting to be run on a CPU:

```
SELECT scheduler_id, current_tasks_count, runnable_tasks_count
FROM sys.dm_os_schedulers
WHERE scheduler_id < 255
```

Did you happen to notice I listed these DMV's twice?

- sys.dm_os_wait_stats

- sys.dm_os_waiting_tasks

These DMV's help to identify the wait stats and types for the activity on your server since the last restart. Wait stats may be one of the most powerful tools you have when it comes to troubleshooting performance issues. Even this simple query:

```
select top 10 *
from sys.dm_os_wait_stats
order by wait_time_ms desc
```

can yield a wealth of information in a short amount of time. While other DBA's are fumbling around to launch SQL Profiler, you could have already isolated the query, what it is waiting for, and propose a possible solution.

Wait Stats

Most people are familiar with the indoor/outdoor thermometers that are sold in stores. These devices let you see the temperature in both places at the same time. They don't really offer an advantage over the traditional method of placing a thermometer outside your window. In fact, unless the probe is placed properly, the reading you get outside may be off by a good amount. In the end, we all check the real temperature outside by opening a door or window and feeling the air on our skin.

Now consider your phone rings and the voice on the other end says "the server is slow." You have a handful of tools at your disposal to look inside the database engine to find out what is happening. In short, you have someone on the outside observing one temperature, and you can look inside for another temperature.

Wait stats are a way for you to feel the air on your skin. They allow for you to immediately know what the issue is, and often times can provide you a solution. They are a hidden gem when it comes to troubleshooting, allowing you to diagnose performance issues in a fraction of the time compared to other tools.

Wait stats can be found through the use of perfmon and the SQLServer:Wait Statistics object. They are also included in the Activity Monitor, having their own section located below the graphs that are displayed. The best usage of wait stats is in the understanding of *wait types*. A list of wait types can be found at: `http://msdn.microsoft.com/en-us/library/ms179984.aspx`. You can find the wait type inside of the sys.dm_os_wait_stats DMV, and you can also find it in the Processes section of the Activity Monitor.

> **TIP:** I would wager a pound of bacon that a majority of the wait types you come across can be solved with some advanced index tuning. Examine some query plans before purchasing new hardware; you'll be doing yourself a favor.

Disk I/O

Wait types that are specific to disk I/O include:

- ASYNC_IO_COMPLETION
- IO_COMPLETION
- IO_RETRY
- PAGEIOLATCH_*
- PAGELATCH_*
- WRITELOG

If you are seeing these wait types as the bulk of your overall waits, then you will most likely want to examine your disk subsystem. Also keep in mind that sometimes issues with disk I/O can be related to memory pressure, so you will want to rule that out before sounding any alarms.

Memory

Wait types that are specific to memory include:

- CMEMTHREAD
- LATCH_*
- LCK_M_*
- LOWFAIL_MEMMGR_QUEUE
- RESOURCE_SEMAPHORE_*
- UTIL_PAGE_ALLOC

If you are seeing these wait types as the bulk of your overall waits, then you will want to investigate the amount of memory that has been allocated to your SQL Server. Locks and latches could be the result of insufficient memory that causes SQL to swap data pages to disk (because it does not have enough memory to store the data in cache), and you could also see some disk I/O issues as well.

CPU

Wait types that are specific to CPU include:

- CXPACKET
- EXCHANGE
- EXECSYNC

There are very few wait types that are dedicated to helping you isolate CPU spikes. The three I have listed are all related to *parallelism*, which can happen during synchronization of a query being run on multiple processors. Essentially, if your query is run in parallel, it gets split onto multiple processors and then needs to be merged back together at the end. This synchronization can be manifested by these wait types.

The quick fix for this situation is to reconfigure the MAXDOP setting for the query, or for the instance as a whole. I always recommend setting the MAXDOP to be one less than the total number of physical processors. This allows for there to be one processor free to handle requests should a parallel query decide to consume the remainder.

SQL Profiler

SQL Profiler allows you to capture the activity running against your database server instance by creating what is called a *trace*. SQL Profiler can be launched either from the Start Menu or from within SQL Server Management Studio. Once started, you configure SQL Profiler to run a trace be selecting various event categories, event classes, columns, and applying filters. You even have the option to select from a handful of default trace templates (see Figure 6–5). For a complete list of SQL Profiler event categories and classes, go to http://msdn.microsoft.com/en-us/library/ms175481.aspx.

The event categories for SQL Profiler are not organized in a way to allow for you to pinpoint one specific category for disk I/O, memory, or CPU. Instead, you have to examine event categories, event classes, and the data columns in order to get the information you need for each potential bottleneck. Think of SQL Profiler as a way to gather details on all the activity against your server, but it will be up to you to analyze the trace output in order to determine where the bottleneck truly lies.

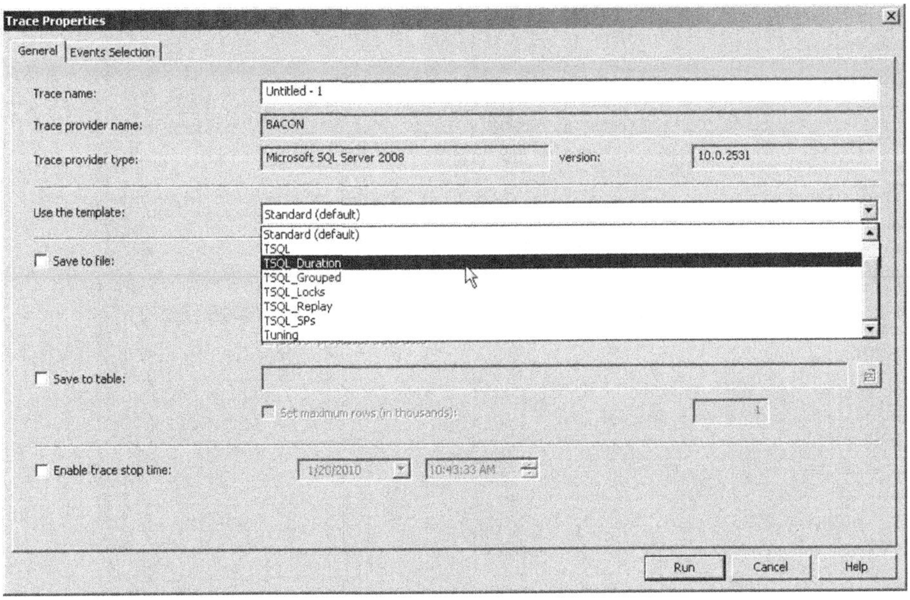

Figure 6–5. *Creating a trace using a default template*

The event categories that are most useful are as follows:

- Cursors
- Database
- Errors and Warnings
- Locks
- Scans
- Stored Procedures
- TSQL

Inside those categories are event classes and those event classes contain data columns. A complete list of available data columns can be found at: http://msdn.microsoft.com/en-us/library/ms190762.aspx. You can also browse them for yourself, if desired. When creating a trace, on the Events Selection tab, simply check off the Show all events and Show all columns boxes (see Figure 6–6). Note that there is a column named CPU, but no column named Memory or disk I/O. That is where your analysis will become valuable as you try to determine the nature of the issue. Many senior DBA's put together a list of default events to capture with a trace file, in the hope that it gives them enough information to begin troubleshooting.

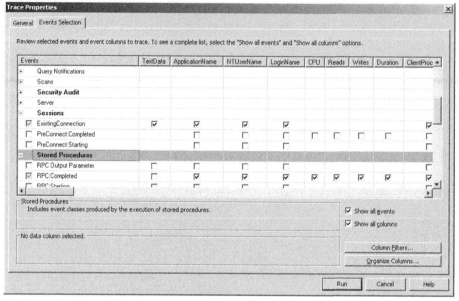

Figure 6–6. *Displaying all events and all data columns*

An example of this would be to capture the RPC:CompletedEvent and SP:BatchCompleted event classes found in the Stored Procedures and TSQL event categories, respectively. Those event classes will allow for you to include data columns for the following:

- ApplicationName
- CPU
- Duration
- LoginName
- Reads
- TextData
- Writes

Since this trace could generate a lot of results it may be worth your time to configure some filters on the data columns. You may want to consider only returning results for statements that have CPU > 500, a duration > 500, reads > 10,000, and writes > 5000, or some combination thereof. You can adjust as necessary in order to have a manageable result set.

As you may have surmised by now, using SQL Profiler to troubleshoot performance issues is a lot more overhead than the other methods discussed. The use of SQL Profiler itself can in turn cause performance issues for the queries that are actively running, so use it with caution on any system in your care. It does allow for a good deal of flexibility in capturing information and when the output is stored in a database table it can allow for easy filtering. Using it to isolate an issue with disk I.O, memory, or CPU is probably more overhead than necessary; it may not lead you to any conclude any one of those potential bottlenecks as your culprit.

> **NOTE:** If you store the results in a database table, you are increasing the activity on the database server. If you don't store the results, you are increasing the memory usage, which is not good if you are already having memory issues, and the increase in disk I/O if you are saving your results to the same drives that your data and log files are using. So choose how you use profiler carefully. —Sylvester Carstarphen.

I have often heard from other senior database administrators that SQL Profiler is not a useful tool for basic troubleshooting. It is useful, however, for those times when you need to capture all the activity (sometimes called a *workload*) hitting your instance. But unless you have a general idea as to where your problem lies, it can be daunting to sift through all of the activity returned. Think of a needle in a haystack and you get the idea.

The Books Online do not even list "troubleshooting" as one of the common uses for SQL Profiler, and yet I still see many people resorting to SQL Profiler as the only tool they want to use to troubleshoot performance issues. A list of scenarios can be found at: http://msdn.microsoft.com/en-us/library/ms190793.aspx. In the end, SQL Profiler is best used when you already have a particular area to focus upon. Otherwise, you are taking a shotgun approach to troubleshooting, which can be quite time consuming.

Disk I/O

Unlike the tools mentioned previously, there is no direct way to use profiler to know if disk I/O is the root cause for the issue you are trying to troubleshoot. There is no event category, event class, or data column that says "check here for disk I/O problems." Compare this to wait types, where you can explicitly find if a query is waiting for disk and decide for yourself which method you would prefer in the middle of the night.

While it is true that you can capture the reads, writes, and duration for queries, these elements alone are not going to tell you if disk I/O is the root cause of your issue. All they can do is point you to using additional tools to take a deeper dive into the trace results. For example, you may find a query with a high duration value but very low reads and writes. You cannot conclude that you have a potential disk I/O issue because that query may have a high duration simply due to the fact that it was a being blocked by other activity.

Memory

SQL Profiler does not offer a direct way to measure potential memory issues. There is no event category, event class, or data column that says "check here for memory problems." Compare this to the Reliability and Performance Monitor where you can configure specific counters to capture memory resource information and you can decide for yourself which method you would prefer to use when someone is standing in your cube and demanding to know how much longer before you fix their problem.

However, you can use SQL Profiler to capture query plans. Inside the Performance Event category you can capture the plans with the Showplan All Event class. You can then examine the query plans and look for operators that are likely to consume memory such as a Hash Match. Personally, I think this is the same as trying to use a hammer to replace a light bulb; it is not the right tool for the task at hand.

CPU

Unlike disk I/O and memory, you can (in theory) use SQL Profiler to troubleshoot CPU issues. Of course, the catch here is that you would need to know that you have CPU issues before you are starting your trace. Otherwise, you are back to the shotgun approach.

So, let's say you suspect a possible CPU issue, or that you know you can use SQL Profiler to look for a possible CPU issue. You can run a trace that contains the CPU data column and filter for a specific CPU duration. Earlier when discussing SQL Profiler, I listed a possible threshold of CPU > 500 along with a handful of categories and classes. I think it is a good idea to focus on the TSQL and Stored Procedure categories as previously mentioned; this will allow for you to examine the queries hitting the server and provide just enough detail for you to focus on a particular application or database that may be adversely affecting the server.

Web Sites

When my children were smaller they would like to ask "Why?" to just about everything, even after I would say "I don't know." This got a little tiring for my wife and me in a short amount of time, so I started answering their questions in a specific way. It went something like this:

Children: "Why?"

Me: "I don't know."

Children: "Why?"

Me: "Because I don't know everything."

Children: "Why?"

Me: "Because no one person can know everything."

Children: "Why?"

Me: "I don't know."

And so we would repeat, eventually they grew tired of asking me "Why?" all the time. Maybe they just grew out of it, but I like to think I helped them through that phase quickly enough. Besides, I was teaching them a very important lesson: no one person knows everything.

Neither do you. As more and more functionality is shoved into SQL Server, get used to not knowing everything about everything. There is going to come a time, fairly quickly, where you will need to go and find an answer. So, where do you begin your search?

Search Engines

My list of search engines is very short. It is either Bing or Google, and nothing else. Either one is a good place to start when you do not know the answer. Input some keywords, or an error message, and start fishing for some answers. I have one colleague who refers to Google as his "junior DBA."

```
http://www.google.com
http://www.bing.com
```

Think of search engines as the 21st century encyclopedia. It is good at letting you read pages that have been printed previously by someone else. Well, except for those rare occasions where a search returns your own blog site and you have forgotten what you wrote years ago.

Forums

Forums are good at interacting with other professionals. Most forums are disconnected conversations. You submit a question and at some point in the future it may or may not be answered. Or you search the forum for similar questions and issues to yours in the hope of inching closer to a resolution.

Here's my short list of forums:

```
http://www.sqlservercentral.com
http://www.msdn.com
http://www.stackoverflow.com
http://www.serverfault.com
http://www.twitter.com
```

SQLServerCentral is one of the top SQL forums available for you to participate in. StackOverflow and ServerFault are also quite good at finding and getting answers. Of course, you can just go right to the source and participate in the MSDN forums as well. Think of forums as a chat room and be mindful of the people you are having a conversation with.

Other forums, most notably the social networking site Twitter, allow for you to interact with others in near real time. If you are connected to other database professionals then there is a good chance you are going to get an answer from your network on Twitter faster than any other type of forum.

Technical Resources

Another group of websites for you to keep handy would be technical resources such as the following two sites:

```
http://www.technet.com
http://www.sqlserverpedia.com
```

These websites and links are similar to having the product manual right in your hands. In some cases, such as SQLServerPedia, it is like having a cheat sheet right at your fingertips.

Chapter 7

Where's the Buffet?

Anyone who knows me also knows I have an affinity for bacon. I like it so much that I am certain it will be my undoing. While it is true that you can add bacon to anything and it will immediately become better, it is also true that too much bacon will clearly lead to health problems. IT professionals make great technical decisions all day long, but when mealtime arrives, we make bad decisions that come back to haunt us. We face long, stressful hours sitting in a chair punctuated by rushed meals of the fastest, most convenient food available. When done in moderation, however, you can have your cake and bacon too.

> **TIP:** Bacon is to food as black is to fashion; it goes with everything.

In this chapter we will discuss the following:

1. How food is the easiest drug of choice

2. How social interactions can lead to poor nutritional choices

3. The need for regular exercise

4. How to avoid letting your career, and life, be cut short

THE MOST IMPORTANT CHAPTER?

by Jonathan Gennick

Do you ever think of your job as being dangerous? You should. We all should. We in the technology industry—book editors included!—can all too easily fall into thinking that we have "safe" jobs. We only drive a desk, right? But we're in grave danger! We're not active enough. We spend all day sitting. Our bodies atrophy. We're at risk from all sorts of coronary disease. There is diabetes to worry about. Have you read about deep vein thrombosis? You get that from sitting too much. Hurt your back lately? Perhaps your core muscles are too flabby to properly protect your back, again due to inactivity.

Think about quality of life. Tom speaks to that near the end of the chapter. He wants to be able to run and play with his kids. I enjoy being active, and I want to continue to be able to get out and hike, ski, mountain bike, and more for as long as I can in life. Yet a few years ago I found myself setting aside cross-country skiing because I found one day that I outweighed the design limits of my skis (I could buy longer skis, but that's not the goal here).

I'm guilty of every one of the poor habits that Tom describes in this chapter. I have lived long enough to experience some of their unwelcome fruits. I have eaten too much, slept too little, and not gotten enough exercise. It is a constant battle to push back, to try and regain ground that I've lost. Don't think you have a dangerous job? Think again!

Food Can Be a Drug

Food is by far the drug of choice for most of us. It is legal, readily available, makes us feel good, and comforts us. We can get together with friends to eat, and we tell ourselves that we can stop eating the unhealthy stuff any time we want, but we never really do.

For example, I love donuts, and wish they came with bacon (either on the side or baked right into the middle like some type of deep-fried calzone). I enjoy having a coffee in the morning and *really* enjoy coffee and beignets. Of course I cannot find beignets most places where I live and work, so I settle for a donut. I can't throw a developer without hitting a donut shop. As much as I love my coffee and donuts, that combination is not something I indulge in every day. I may eat donuts with my coffee once a week, because I understand the need for moderation.

> **TIP:** Moderation and balance are key. You can eat whatever you want to eat, providing you do so in moderation and follow a balanced diet.

The next time you head over to the vending machine for a quick fix of something crispy, cheesy, and salty, stop and think to yourself about why you are buying that snack. Chances are you will find yourself eating not from hunger, but from emotional eating or unconscious eating.

Emotional Eating

This is often the result of some emotional trigger. It can be brought about by stress that is a result of your current job function. For example, your company may be going through layoffs and you have been asked to help manage the project, meaning you will be eliminating the jobs of people you have worked with for years. Or you may simply have a colleague who treats you will little respect and is very demanding. The stress that is put upon you can directly lead to emotional eating.

NOTE: The problem of emotional eating is well-recognized in medicine. The Mayo Clinic has an excellent article on the topic at www.mayoclinic.com/health/weight-loss/MH00025. A quick Google search on the term "emotional eating" will turn up a plethora of other articles for you to feast upon.

When you are eating emotionally, you are using food as a way to control your mood. It could be something as simple as a way to combat boredom. Because you do not like to be bored, you start to think about some ice cream. Now that you are thinking about ice cream, you are no longer bored, and before you know it you are having yourself a triple scoop of Rocky Road.

Emotional eating is a pattern that you do not want to fall into. You swear you will not eat another pound of bacon for breakfast and then you do it again the next day. Your colleague or manager treats you poorly in front of the office and you reach for a bag of chips. You find yourself eating *when you are not even hungry*.

Emotional eating can be difficult to overcome. The first step to solving any problem is to first identify that the problem exists. Once you have done that, the next step could be something simple, like keeping a food diary of what you eat throughout the day. Or it could be more complex, like seeking the help of a therapist. In the end, you need to be more focused on your well-being and less likely to react to the emotional eating.

Unconscious Eating

Unconscious eating happens when you are not aware that you are putting food into your mouth. It sounds silly, right? I mean, *how can you not know you are eating?* It is not a matter of not knowing that you are eating, it is more a matter that you are not aware of how much or what you are eating.

The classic example is movie theater popcorn. Most of the time the popcorn at the theater is made well in advance (sometimes days in advance) and stored in big plastic bags until it is taken out, placed under heat lamps, and served to the public. If you were to be given a bowl of that popcorn and a bowl of freshly popped popcorn, the difference in the taste would be quite noticeable. And yet when you go to watch a movie you are content to eat the entire bucket of stale popcorn instead of demanding something fresh. Why? Because *you are eating unconsciously.*

You are distracted by the movie. Your focus is not on your food, it is somewhere else. As a result, you continue to shovel popcorn down your throat until it is all gone. Same thing for eating in front of the television, or . . .

Your computer screen.

Yes, it is true. Sitting at your desk watching your computer screen all day is enough of a distraction for you to start down the path that leads to unconscious eating. Don't believe me? Get up out of your chair, leave your cube, and start taking notice of the physical appearance of others in your department. My guess is that more than half of them are overweight. And they are probably also doing exactly what you do all day; sitting at their desk staring at a computer screen.

> **TIP:** Getting out of your cube is a good idea anyway. Go ahead and stretch your legs for a few minutes. Walk up a flight of stairs when you have the chance.

And for those that are not distracted and eating, you will find people who are simply procrastinating and using food as a distraction. Weird as this may sound, there are many times when you may be procrastinating about a task and find yourself getting up and reaching for something to snack on. Heck, since I started this chapter I have eaten bacon and potato chips, and had some ice tea. Not exactly a salad, is it?

Overcoming Bad Habits

How do you combat emotional or unconscious eating? As noted before, the first thing you need to do is to recognize the problem is happening. From there you will have different ways to overcome the bad eating habits. My favorite would happen to be the food diary. You simply write down everything you eat throughout the day. No matter how big or small, you write it down. By the time you get to the afternoon and you see a long list, it is easy to understand where and how the extra calories are getting added to your diet.

Another little trick I like to use is to surround myself with healthier options. I will take carrot sticks or an orange to have as an afternoon snack. Some days I have an apple before lunch. This helps me to understand that if I start to reach for something later on that I am not doing so because I am hungry; I have already had a snack.

> **TIP:** Other snack items I like include grapes, almonds, and wasabi peas. And popcorn—I love popcorn—and a snack-size bag is just the right size.

There are also going to be times where you decide to skip a meal, most likely lunch. Skipping meals will cause your metabolism to slow, lower your energy, and reduce your ability to focus. Worse than all that is that you will be more inclined to start snacking, so it is always a good tip to check your calendar; if you know you are pressed for time, then pack yourself some healthy snacks.

SET AN ALARM

by Brent Ozar

Don't be afraid to set calendar timers to force yourself to have a small snack at midday and again at mid-afternoon. I've got alarms set at 10:00 a.m. and 2:00 p.m. to force myself to eat a 100-calorie snack twice a day. That way, at lunch and dinnertime, I'm less hungry. And being less hungry, I'm less tempted to stuff that entire burrito into my mouth in one sitting. If you let yourself get starved, then you may overeat at mealtime.

Still another trick is to drink some water. It is a good idea to have some water right before a meal, as it will help to fill your stomach before you start eating. Most people tend to not recognize the clues that their stomach is full until after they have overeaten. By taking water before your meal (that's water, not soda!), you help to reduce the chance that you are going to overeat.

Social Gatherings

At some point in your professional career you will find yourself in a social setting with your coworkers, and food will be nearby. Trust me, it will happen. It could be something quite informal, such as the sharing of a birthday cake for someone in the department. Or it could be something more formal such as a holiday gathering. No matter what the setting, a few things will remain constant: you, them, and food.

In all cases you need to be prepared to make smart choices. One piece of birthday cake would be more than enough. So would one cocktail-sized plate of wings at a happy hour, or just one drink at that same happy hour. The trouble is that when you are surrounded by tasty treats and people to have conversations with, it is all too easy to overindulge. These moments are not limited to special events, either—they can happen during your regular routine as well.

Breakfast

We all have a breakfast routine. Good or bad, it is something we tend to follow as we start our workday. And a majority of people start their day with a cup of coffee with friends.

Coffee. Caffeine. Cream. Sugar.

All good things, right? Not really, no. I doubt I need to inform you about the ills of too much sugar or cream in your diet. Many people tend to believe that the real problem with coffee is the caffeine. And they would be wrong. It is the cream and the sugar that will be worse for you over time.

While you may feel that you cannot function without your cup of coffee in the morning, stop and think about someone who is addicted to cocaine—who needs just a little bump to get to the next one. Sure, caffeine is a drug, and I can hear you already telling me, "No, it is not like that, not at all." Yes, it is, actually. You may not be pawning your DVD player in order to get enough scratch to order a venti triple quad latte, but the idea is very much the same; if you are one of those that absolutely needs to have a cup of coffee in the morning, then you have an addiction.

TIP: The first step in overcoming your addiction is to admit you have one.

If you still feel that you need to have that cup of coffee, then start thinking about switching to decaf. You can ease into it—just order your coffee for the next two weeks by saying "half-decaf," and the barista will be happy to accommodate. You can break your addiction in a short time. Do the same with the cream and sugar—start using less until you just about drink your coffee black, like you should be drinking it. Why?

> *Because the thing you really need to be aware of is that your coffee is just a vehicle to get the cream and sugar into your body.*

I knew a man once who drank his coffee black. I asked him how he could drink coffee without even some cream to temper it, and his reply has stuck with me to this day: "Would you pour cream and sugar into a glass of 20-year-old Scotch?" I stared blankly at him and replied softly, "No." He responded with, "Then why would you want to ruin a perfectly good cup of coffee by pouring that junk in it?"

Exactly. If coffee is a part of your breakfast routine, you need to be mindful of the effects it will have on you over time. This can be difficult if you are accustomed to heading down to grab a cup with your friends in the morning. I enjoy taking a walk with friends every morning to get a cup myself, but I do my best to be mindful of what I am putting into my body. After the first cup of coffee each morning, put the coffee cup away, and place a full bottle of water on your desk. Instead of unconsciously drinking the coffee, you'll be unconsciously drinking something that doesn't have ill effects.

Do not let your breakfast routine get in the way of making good choices. Skip the sausage, egg, and cheese biscuit and frappuccino. Try to have some black decaf coffee or tea and an egg on English muffin (no cheese or sausage) once a week when you head out with your friends.

Then make that same healthy choice twice a week. Before you know it, you will be having breakfast with your friends and not slowly poisoning yourself to death or adding a few extra pounds with each passing year.

Lunch

How many times has someone stopped by your desk and said something akin to the following:

"I'm heading out to the local high-caloric sandwich shop; can I get you something?" You want to say no, but you don't normally eat there often and think of this as a treat. You place your order, finish your double chicken cutlet, and promise yourself to go for a walk when you get home (you won't).

"A vendor's taking all of us to Oversized Burritos, and the ingredients are all organic." Organic doesn't necessarily mean healthy. Raw butter can be completely organic, but it will clog your arteries faster than you can say "Paula Deen." In addition, just because something's free doesn't mean you need to eat a lot of it.

Or perhaps instead of one person heading out, someone stops by and says, "We're heading down to the Chinese place that pretends to be a healthy Thai place, but everything is deep fried there anyway. Want to come along?" You want to say no, but you don't normally eat there often and think of this as a treat. You get up and head out to grab a bite to eat with some friends and promise to go for a jog later when you get home (you won't).

I want to make one thing very clear: *none of us is as dumb as all of us*. It is amazing to watch a group of people make poor decisions that they wouldn't make as individuals. It happens all the time, and not just with food. There is something about group mentality that can make smart people look less than smart.

It can be difficult to turn down the chance to be socially interactive with your coworkers. And you do not want to be the only one in the group that insists on heading to a place that has a menu selection that did not have parents. But you do need to be mindful that when the situations come up, that you have some options.

For example, you could reply with, "I brought my lunch, but I wouldn't mind going for a walk if you are planning on bringing your lunch back here." See? You get to talk a walk and have some social interaction, but you still get to eat the healthier lunch.

What? You did not bring lunch? Well then, try this response instead: "Oh, I was planning on going to the place right next door; I will walk with you anyway and grab a bite at the place I was going to eat that won't be giving me a heart episode by the time I am 39." See how easy that is? You can still grab your lunch at the healthier place, and you still get to walk with your coworkers. A venerable win-win if there ever was one.

The end result should be that you make your best effort to avoid unhealthy options simply because you are with a group.

Happy Hours

Nothing says peer pressure like a happy hour. Getting together with your coworkers for a few pints of lager after work can lead to an extra few thousand calories as you have a handful of pints and appetizers. If there are a few executives around, it can only add to the pressure if they order you a round. After all, no one wants to tell the big boss no. Chances are you would rather have the drink because it would give you the opportunity to spend a few minutes having a conversation. Trust me, if the boss is buying drinks, chances are you are not counting calories. Even more so if there is a group of you there, because you already know that *none of us is as dumb as all of us*.

How do you avoid this scenario? Well, you could always turn down the offer to attend the function. Of course you may feel that it is important to be social. Well, why not attend for just a while—say, 30 minutes—and then excuse yourself? You would seem to get the best of both worlds there. You get to socialize with your coworkers and you get to avoid all the extra unhealthy eating that is bound to happen as people have a few extra drinks.

> **TIP:** If you feel that your job depends upon your participation in such events, then you will either need to take steps to avoid the peer pressure, accept that you will gain weight, or find a new job.

And if you are heading to the happy hour, you should grab yourself some water before you head out. Filling your stomach with some water will trick your body into thinking that it has had food already, and you will be less inclined to snack (and hopefully less inclined to drink).

Traveling

Traveling for business can also lead to poor nutritional choices. You are in an unfamiliar area, you end up ordering from room service, and you are able to use an expense account. It all adds up to a lot of extra calories as you decide to try something different. And why not? If you are on the road, why not treat yourself to trying something a little different than your normal dinner of lentil loaf and a spinach salad?

The thing to keep in mind when traveling is moderation. You want to have a triple bacon cheeseburger? Fine, but do not make it your dinner every night. Make sure you drink plenty of water and go out of your way for a healthier option the other nights. You may find it hard to stick to a routine because you may not have a routine, unless you travel frequently.

I like to rent a car when I travel because then I have the option to head to a local grocery store. Not only does it save money, but I find that I will have the widest possible variety of meal selections. Sure, I do not have a kitchen, but a lot of supermarkets these days have prepared meals that I can sample, or a salad bar, and maybe even some sushi. When you travel, you want things to be as similar to home as possible.

When you are home, your meals are usually made from items you have purchased at your local supermarket, right? If so, then why not have supermarket food on the road as well? Even if you are in town for just two nights, you can stop by a supermarket and pick up some items for breakfast, lunch, and dinner that would be better nutritional choices than anything on the room service menu.

> **TIP:** You can find lots of great traveling tips online these days. As with any advice, you need to try things for yourself to see what works best.

The harder part when traveling would be the temptation to head out for a bite to eat with people you see infrequently. Maybe you will grab lunch with a couple of coworkers and dinner with someone else. Or meet up for breakfast at a local pancake palace. It can be all too easy to find yourself eating out all the time with all sorts of different people.

It can be difficult, but it is not impossible to make good choices and put yourself into good situations when traveling. Sometimes it takes a bit of creativity. Almost always it takes dedication. Whatever it takes, do it. Don't give up on yourself. You're worth the effort.

Exercise

I know that when most people hear the word *exercise*, they think about something difficult and strenuous. They imagine endless jogs, lifting weights, swimming laps, being out of breath, and sweating through their clothes even when they get back to the office. They also imagine aching muscles, sore backs, and that they don't have enough time in the day for any of that.

While the above is certainly true for the majority forms of exercise, it is not always the case. There is a way for you to increase your activity level without the sweat and strain associated with hitting the gym during your lunch hour. And it is something you have been doing almost your whole life: walking.

OR NOT WALKING

by Jonathan Gennick

Tom is of course spot-on to recommend walking as good exercise. It is wonderful exercise, and requires no special skill or equipment. I live in a small town, and I take advantage of that to run many errands on foot.

But another point of view is to find something fun that you enjoy doing, that is active. More than walking even, I like to ride bikes—always have, ever since my receiving my very first one as young child. I'm not talking about exercise bikes that don't go anywhere. Those bore me to tears. But put me on a bike that moves, and I'm good and willing to go for a long time. I like bikes so much that I even ride in winter, on ice, using studded tires imported from Finland.

Find something active that motivates you. If it's something you spend all day wishing you could do, so much the better. Spend—no, invest—the money in whatever good equipment and gear you need. Exercise is a lot easier and comes more naturally when the activity is something you're passionate about.

Extra Steps

There are a handful of ways to incorporate walking into your life. You could get a dog and go for a walk in the morning or the evening. Or you could walk with your children after dinner. You could even take a walk during your lunchtime, perhaps taking a stroll around the block. What you are really looking for are extra steps in your day or week.

One place to find extra steps is to park farther away from your office. There are roughly 20 working days in a month. If you park 50 feet farther away from your office, then you must walk 100 extra feet each day. Multiply that by 20 working days and you will have walked 2,000 extra feet in 1 month, and 24,000 extra feet in 1 year—that is almost 5 miles of walking.

Another place to find extra steps are, well, steps! Take the stairs when you have the chance, especially for only one or two flights. Your heart will thank you later.

Walking is one of the most popular forms of exercise in the world. A few steps here and there add up over time; you just need to find where the extra steps are in your daily routine.

If you want to go to an extreme measure, then you should look into the Treadmill Desk (www.treadmill-desk.com). The idea is simple: you walk on a treadmill going 1 mile per hour while you work at your desk. You can burn up to 100 extra calories per hour and lose weight while you work.

The Need for Regular Exercise

Part of your daily or weekly routine should include regular exercise. Regular exercise will reduce your stress levels, keep you in good health, and increase your energy level. Yet despite all of the documented benefits of regular exercise, many people do not make the effort to incorporate it into their daily routines. There always seems to be an excuse that falls into one of two camps: too much work and not enough time.

If you are looking for the easy way out of doing regular exercise, then claiming to have too much work is the excuse for you. Everyone has more work than they can handle these days, especially a DBA. We are expected to be available at all hours and find ourselves always trying to get caught up on alerts and even configure new ways to be proactive in order to maintain a stable environment. But you must find the time. It is important for you to carve out some time, in some way, to raise your activity level. You can start small by taking extra steps every day and work your way up toward regular walks.

In addition to having too much work, you can also find yourself simply short on time. Perhaps your commute is slightly longer than average and those extra minutes in the car provide you with an excuse as to why you do not have enough time in the day to care for yourself. The only advice I can give someone who claims to have no time is to write down all your activities and see how long they are taking. You may find some extra time in your day by evaluating where your time is being spent currently.

> **TIP:** Regular exercise can also be a great way to network with other professionals, even some within your own company.

Sleep

Chances are you have heard about the benefits of having at least 8 hours of uninterrupted sleep per night. In case you have not yet heard, then let me be the first to tell you: *you need to get some rest*. Whenever I get too little rest during the night, I often find myself grabbing an extra-large cup of coffee the next morning. The entire day seems to be a little foggier than normal, I end up crashing around dinnertime, and I get a second wind and find myself working late again the next night. And the next day the cycle repeats.

Many of the DBAs I know are people who are driven to become better at their careers. The more they are driven, the more sacrifices they will be asked to make. One of the easiest things that people tend to sacrifice is sleep. They will stay up an extra 30 minutes to finish a chapter or tweak some T-SQL, and then the 30 minutes becomes an hour, and before they know any better it is 2:00 a.m. and they need to be up in a few hours.

Not getting enough rest on a regular basis can lead to a host of problems, the least of which is falling asleep while driving. Or it could be physiological, such as a backache, which I often get when I have not had enough sleep.

If you find yourself falling into bad sleep habits, a simple way to get back on track is to go to bed a little bit earlier each night. Think of it as a bank; invest some extra time up front and you can reap the dividends later on.

Another reason to make certain you are getting enough rest is because of the times you will be needed to work on short rest. For example, when you are needed to perform some emergency repair work at 3:00 a.m., you need to be as alert as possible in order to do the job well. If you have not been getting enough sleep on a regular basis, you will find yourself sluggish in the middle of the night, which could lead to easy mistakes being made at the worst possible time.

> **TIP:** For more details and information on the importance of sleep, check out `www.apa.org/topics/whysleep.html`.

Calories

Counting calories is not the same as nutrition or exercise. Many people go out of their way to avoid certain foods in an effort to reduce their calories. My favorite is the ordering of diet soda with a meal. Although the person would be better off with water or juice, somehow they think that because a diet soda has fewer calories than a regular one, they are doing themselves a favor. To them I have one thing to say: *diet soda can make you eat more*.

> **TIP:** Check out all the gory details on exercise, carbohydrates, diet soda, and your brain at `http://jp.physoc.org/content/587/8/1779.full`, which presents a study published in the Journal of Physiology; and at `www.menstuff.org/issues/byissue/dietsoda.html`. Also check out the article "Energy Drinks Work in Mysterious Ways," at `www.medicalnewstoday.com/articles/146062.php`, which does a good job of explaining the results of the original study.

The effect of eating more because of ordering a diet soda is far worse than the extra calories you would get with a regular soda. After all, would you rather have an extra 100 calories now or an extra few hundred extra calories later on? The bottom line is if you feel the need to order a diet soda, just order some water instead.

I will agree that being mindful of calories is a good thing. If you are looking for some overall weight loss, then there are two things to keep in mind: reduce your caloric intake and raise your activity level. We already discussed some of the ways to increase your activity levels over time. Imagine the benefits you will get should you start being mindful of calories as well. Some people have even suggested that one of the secrets to a longer life is to eat fewer calories.

Life Is Good, but It's Better with Bacon

I work in an IT department. The hours can be demanding, the job often doesn't conform to a rigid schedule, and it requires me to work many weekends. When my daughter was born, I decided that I needed to lift weights for the next 18 years so that I could be ready in case she decided to start dating someone on the football team. After my son was born, I realized I could stop lifting weights and just train him instead. But another goal came to mind. The goal was to be able to play in the yard with my children and (1) not be short of breath and (2) not risk a heart attack, no matter how much bacon I may have consumed.

I have spent the past few years doing what I can to attain that goal. I started jogging, began to pay attention to how much and what I was eating, and started making a real effort to have the best possible work/life balance. I am able to play soccer with my children, chase them on their bikes, and just have fun in the backyard. Every day is Father's Day. Never mind having my career cut short due to poor nutrition—I do not want my *life* cut short.

Think about this scenario: you wake up in the morning, get yourself ready for work, and head out in your car for your morning commute. You do not bother with breakfast while at home, because you grab a cup of cream and sugar (and some coffee) with some coworkers most mornings. Unfortunately traffic is unusually heavy this morning, and it takes too long to get to the office.

Your poor nutritional choices lead to you becoming light-headed, and you lose control of the car and head into a ditch. Later on you find out how difficult it is to administer servers from the emergency room with a broken arm.

And that's why I always drive around with an extra donut in my glove compartment.

If you do not believe that the preceding scenario is possible, then try this one: you are at your desk finishing up an extra-large sesame chicken dinner from that Thai place down the street that you think is healthier because it is Thai food and not Chinese food, but it's really all the same. You fall asleep about an hour after lunch as if it were Thanksgiving all over again and you end up drooling all over your desk. Your boss stops by and snaps a quick picture on his Blackberry. You have no idea about the photo until your next performance review when he shows it to you and then says, "Now…about that raise you won't be getting this year."

Perhaps you are not the type to fall asleep after a large meal. At least, not that you remember, right? Well, let's try one more: your steady diet with a minimal amount of leafy green items has led you to have low enough iron content in your blood to make you anemic. You are heading up to your office in the elevator one morning and you get a sudden nosebleed. You try to stop the bleeding but your blood does not clot as quickly as it should. The doors open, your boss is standing there, you bleed all over his shoes, and you make the elevator and office floor look like a crime scene.

Still think these scenarios are impossible? Well, they aren't. Many people are either anemic or borderline anemic due to the lack of iron brought about by poor nutrition. People fall asleep after large meals. And lots of drivers lose their concentration; there is no real way to know how many accidents are caused by low blood sugar, but I would be willing to wager that a good number are.

I know that it can be difficult to strike a perfect balance between your work schedule and your personal schedule. And often you will find yourself using work as an excuse to avoid taking time for yourself. But you need to make the time for yourself, and one way to do that is to be mindful of what you are eating.

MAKE THE TIME!

by Jonathan Gennick

It is so important to make the time. Your job will eat you alive if you let it. Taking care of ourselves would be easier if the penalties were more immediate. Imagine if your boss came to you saying, "Will you stay late and have a heart attack in order to get that new database created?" Wow! It would be easy to say no to that request. What's hard is that each sacrifice is so small, so incremental. Taking care of yourself involves taking a very long-term view.

One of the easiest ways to be mindful of what you are eating is to keep track by writing it down on a piece of paper. If pen and paper are too rustic for your liking, then you can always get an application for your iPhone that allows you to record your meals and calculate your calories.

Writing down or tracking your meals will also help you to be mindful of, or eliminate, snacking. The bag of chips and can of soda in the middle of the afternoon is adding 350 empty calories to your diet each day. There are roughly 3,500 calories in a pound of body fat. With 20 working days in a month, that would equate to 2 pounds of body fat per month or 20 pounds of body fat per year. And if you think it is unreasonable to believe that someone is eating chips and soda for a snack every day, then just consider it to be done once a week, and that the 20 pounds gets tacked on over five years instead.

Believe me, five years can go by quickly. The weight will go on very slowly, but it will go on. And despite it taking years to go on, many people think they can take it all off in a matter of weeks. As a result, they get frustrated with any change in their daily routine that does not have immediate results.

The point is that you need to start putting yourself first; stop making excuses and start being responsible for your health as if your life depends on it, *because it does*.

Chapter 8

Training, Get You Some of That

Stop for a moment and reflect on how far you have come to this point. You wanted to become a DBA, you found your opportunity, you have built up relationships with colleagues, and you are effectively running the ship at this point. Along the way you have noticed that certain aspects of your environment tend to shift over time. One shift is, of course, new releases of SQL Server. Even applying a hotfix to SQL Server could provide you with an unexpected learning opportunity.

Many people simply do not consider training an important part of their life as a DBA. If you want to survive as a DBA, then you need to be able to quickly adapt to changing circumstances. You need to be aware of ideas and concepts that are on the horizon. In short, you need training, and that training is an ongoing function that never stops.

> **TIP:** Training is the point at which education and motivation meet.

When times get tough, training budgets are one of the first things to get their funding cut. This can make it difficult for you to convince your management to send you away for a day or two in order to keep your skills sharp. You must find a way to present a business case that is rock-solid; get them to understand that there will be a substantial return on their investment.

Training is more than just sitting in a classroom for three to five days and listening to an instructor offer up information from a study guide prepared by someone else. Effective training is much more than that; it is something that becomes a part of your everyday routine. You may be good at what you do right now, but you are far from perfect (trust me), and if you do not spend some of your time following the latest industry trends, then you will be left behind like a dinosaur trapped in a tar pit.

In this chapter, we will discuss the following:

1. Reasons for training
2. Training resources
3. Building your case

Reasons for Training

Think of a high school basketball program. You would have a varsity team, a junior varsity (JV) team, and a freshman team. Each team would have practices, and the natural progression of a player would be from the freshman team to the JV team and then on to varsity. But who decides when a player is ready to move upward? The varsity coach, of course, who is managing the entire program and constantly evaluating the players daily, would be the one responsible for that decision.

At the start of the season, the coach will put in the base set of offensive and defensive plays that the team will use for the season. These plays will be based upon the individual players' strengths; however, during the course of the season, new plays will be put into the system in order to make certain the team remains competitive, which makes their fans happy.

> **TIP:** Keeping fans happy is *always* a priority, no matter if you are coaching a high school basketball team or administering the database servers for a large corporation.

Now compare that to an IT department. You have a person that serves as the head of IT (your varsity coach) and is responsible for evaluating the employees as part of an overall professional development program. Depending upon the performance of an employee, it could be desirable to have them placed into a new role. Or it could be that a new system is being brought in house and certain employees will be shifted over to be dedicated to working with the new system. At the end of the day, the head of IT is going to make the moves that she feels will provide the business with the highest level of satisfaction.

With regard to training, the two scenarios are the same. In each case you have people changing roles or positions, you have new systems being put into place, you have people evaluating the employees and players, and you want your customers to be happy. We could therefore say that there are four good reasons for companies to offer training: for professional development, for when people change roles, for new systems, and for customer satisfaction. Each of those reasons will result in benefits for the employee as well as for the business.

Professional Development

Professional development can have many meanings to many people. For some, it means career growth. For others it may simply be another way to describe their annual performance review. And still others may think of professional development as their career track within a company.

The results of annual reviews could lead a company to institute a training program. For example, an employee may be told that they are lacking in a core set of necessary skills for their position. The company may then see fit to offer some training to that employee in an effort to help them with their development. Or the evaluation could point out that the employee is excelling in a certain area and it might be a good idea to offer training in order to enhance some existing skills.

> **TIP:** A proper review should also include a training plan for the upcoming year.

Training should be a part of any professional development program. If training is not listed on any official review or professional development program, then make your own plan that includes training. And training does not need to mean time away from the office in a classroom located in some exotic location. I will list out for you later in this chapter many of the training resources and options you have available.

Good companies will offer strong professional development opportunities. Note that this does not mean that the company has positions of advancement to offer; in most cases they will not. But what good companies will do is make certain their employees are given opportunities to pursue positions they enjoy. Sometimes those positions exist and sometimes they are created. But without training it will be difficult for the IT director to be able to evaluate the employee's growth potential. What you want to do is use your training to enhance your skills and in turn help to demonstrate your increased value to your employer.

Changing Roles

Your desires and motivations will change over time. As a result it will often be necessary to consider changing roles. Sometimes this could mean a promotion, but it could also mean a lateral move. Perhaps you have been working in the QA department and want to move into a junior administration role. Companies that have training programs in place allow for this changing of roles easily; otherwise it would be very difficult to allow for internal growth opportunities. And if there are no internal growth opportunities for the employees, then low morale could be a result.

I know of many database professionals who started out as straightforward DBAs and are now more involved with business intelligence, database development, or even SAN administration. As your desires change over time, look for opportunities to work with your boss to get some additional knowledge and training so that if new roles are created, you will have an opportunity to fill that role.

Piloting New Systems

Systems come and go, especially in the IT sector. When new systems come into your shop, your company is going to need someone to administer and support them. This can be done by (1) training existing employees, (2) hiring new employees or contractors with the necessary experience, or (3) doing nothing.

Doing nothing will lead to poor administration and support, which will lead to poor customer satisfaction. Hiring new employees is an option, but may be cost prohibitive. Most of the time the best course of action is to train current employees to work with the new system.

Customer Satisfaction

Companies should always be looking to increase customer satisfaction. After all, if they alienate their customers to the point that no customers remain, then they will not be in business very long. Training programs have the ability to increase customer satisfaction as an end result. How? By improving the morale of the employees. When you create a positive work environment, you allow for the opportunity to create a positive customer experience as well.

> **TIP:** While you should enjoy your work, there is a reason it is called work and not "happy fun play time." It is not your employer's responsibility to keep you entertained. It is their responsibility to keep you focused and productive.

Think about places you may have worked where office morale was low. What was it like to be a customer of that company? Was it a positive experience? Chances are that most interactions between those customers and your company were not very positive. Now I cannot pinpoint that bad interaction on the lack of a decent training program; what I am saying is that one reason for instituting a training program would be in order to have higher customer satisfaction as a result.

Employee Benefits

There is little question that there are lots of benefits to the employees that are receiving the training. You get to increase your skill set, make new contacts, expand your network, and essentially increase your value to the company, because no company wants to lose an employee that they invest training dollars on.

There are a lot of other benefits that employees receive through training that many people do not consider because they are focused only on the short term. But when looking at the larger picture, you can start to see a host of ancillary benefits.

Job Satisfaction

When you are involved in a training program, it can energize you and give you some confidence in your abilities, which then boils over into your overall job satisfaction. You become more confident in your daily duties as a result of training. Better yet, your training allows you to take on new responsibilities. While most people enjoy some routine in their lives, they also enjoy a dose of variety. As you gain confidence, you enjoy your job more, leading to increased job satisfaction.

Employee Motivation

Training can lead to an increase in your motivation. In addition to the confidence and increase in job satisfaction, you will often find yourself motivated to do more. That extra bit of training may be the difference between having employees that are just punching the clock to having employees that come in early and stay a little late.

Process Efficiencies

Probably one of the least obvious employee training benefits is the increase in efficiency that can result. An employee could find ways to take a 30-minute task down to a 5-minute task. As a DBA you may find ways to performance tune queries that can cut your tuning time from days to hours. That saves time, and we all know that time is money, right?

Think about some of the recent tools at your disposal for administration. PowerShell, Operations Manager, and Policy-Based Management. Each one is still fairly new, and each one is designed to improve your efficiency at being a DBA. With some training, you will be able to discover new ways to do some of your current tasks with a method that is easier to maintain.

Time Management

When you become more efficient, you start to save time. What you also get is the ability to better manage your time. How many times have you been expected to drop everything and respond to a critical issue? Then, after responding, you do your best to dissect the problem and are then badgered for constant updates: "How much longer before you fix the problem?"

With training, those issues take less time to resolve, giving you the ability to effectively manage critical issues and continue to get your regular work done. In short, you have the ability to manage your time better.

Communication Skills

Even if you are not attending a class designed to work on communication (or "soft") skills, you can see an increase in those skills regardless. Through training you get the opportunity to interact with others in an environment outside of the office. After the training is complete and you start applying your new skills to your current position, you will then start having the opportunity to be interacting with different people inside your office.

> **TIP:** Your communication skills will improve in time, but only if you look to improve upon them. This can be done be simply reviewing prior conversations and seeing if you could have done something better.

In most cases your training will give you the opportunity to share your new skills with others in your office, particularly with other team members. This is certainly a chance to improve upon your soft skills—a chance you may not been given without having been offered the training to begin with.

Business Benefits

Despite knowing that training has benefits for employees, some companies do not invest as much time and energy into training their employees as they should. One reason for this is that the company does not fully understand the benefits of training their employees. If you are able to learn, understand, and communicate the benefits effectively, then you have a chance at convincing your company to help defray some (or possibly all) of the hard dollar costs.

Everyone needs training, regardless of their level of experience. Everyone has room for improvement. The improvement could be something dramatic, such as going from being a novice to someone highly skilled. Or it could be that someone who is highly skilled wants to hone those skills even further in order to stay ahead of the competition, such as an Olympic athlete.

The truth is that training offers not only employee benefits but business benefits. Companies should understand and recognize that having an ongoing training structure in place is a necessary part of their business.

When it comes to training programs, most people tend to think that the only person receiving a benefit is the person receiving the training. While it is true that the employee is getting a direct benefit, it is also true that the employer also receives a benefit. Some of these benefits we have already seen, such as the increase in customer satisfaction that is brought about by providing better customer service. Or the increase in productivity that results from increased efficiency. But there are a handful of other benefits to the business that can be directly attributed to training.

Improved Morale

We already saw that training can lead to an increase in job satisfaction. And employees who feel satisfied in their jobs are vital to ensuring that office morale stays high. It may not be practical to train everyone, so the IT manager is going to have to find a way to justify and rotate the training needs of the department. When done correctly, training can have dramatic effects on office morale.

Reduced Turnover

Employees who feel satisfied by their jobs are less likely to leave. Employee retention is important for two reasons. First, you want consistency in your ability to support the business. Second, you do not want to go through the time and expense to find new employees. Given the choice between spending tens of thousands of dollars to find new employees or offering some training, it would be cheaper if your company offered some periodic training.

Reduced Risk

Training can be effective in the reduction of risk. The risk in question can vary; it could be making certain that everyone has sexual harassment training, for example. Or you may want to reduce your risk with regard to Sarbanes-Oxley compliance. I cannot think of one employee that desires to go to a training class on Sarbanes-Oxley compliance, but I can think of many businesses that would see a benefit from sending their employees to such classes.

Staying Competitive

Training employees offers a business the ability to stay competitive in their industry. They have the chance to take advantage of new technologies before a competitor, for example. In some industries it is vital to stay on the cutting edge of technology; in others it is vital to be able to use existing technology but simply be the first one to get a specific product to market before someone else. The business benefit for this aspect of training dollars is potentially the most lucrative.

Training Resources

There are many options available for individuals or companies looking to get started on a training program. The first step is to identify the desired end result; what do you hope to get from your training? More importantly than *what you get* from your training is *what you can take* from your training. If you are going to expect to have things handed to you or done for you, then you are going to be disappointed.

No matter what your budget, you can find some level of training to suit your needs. There are lots of free options for training (web sites) and lots of slightly-more-expensive-than-free choices (professional trainer). When making arrangements for a training program, you should be mindful of each option and its associated strengths and weaknesses.

TIP: Do some research when hiring a trainer or attending a class. Make certain you are getting a reputable trainer.

Notice that the options I discuss are a mixture of self-help and organized training classes. That is because any good training program is going to incorporate more than one option. If you are waiting around for someone else to put together your training for you, then you are most likely going to be left behind. You absolutely need to take control of your own career development; grab the self-help options when you are able.

Web Sites

The Internet offers a lot of reference material for training. As a DBA you may be focused on SQL Server training options, but even if you are looking for something different—perhaps some general professional development training—you should be able to find a web site through a search from your favorite search engine. Participation in forums, newsgroups, and even Twitter can offer valuable training material.

Pros: Most are free, but some charge for content. Web sites allow for you to conduct training on your schedule; typically you do not need to be online at a particular day and time. Forums and newsgroups are often a good way to connect with other professionals and share experiences. Some companies such as Microsoft and Oracle offer a lot of training materials for free with the hope that they can persuade professionals such as yourself to use their products.

Cons: You get what you pay for. You need to be mindful that there are crazy people out there posting responses to forum questions, and there are people posting humorous answers as a joke that you might not get. It can be hard to distinguish between sites that offer quality content and those that do not, but one way to start is to look at each author's experience. Don't take the word of an uncredentialed stranger when it comes to your databases. And don't believe that paying a premium for content means you can trust the material any more than a free web site; I have seen lots of mistakes on web sites that charge for content.

Self-Training

In addition to the self-training that you can get from web sites, blogs, and podcasts, you can also simply get started on a side project that will allow you to learn something new. Perhaps your company needs to institute transaction log shipping and you have never done that before. Consider this your opportunity to teach yourself something new.

Pros: There is no better way to learn than by doing. And with self-training you often are doing something that already has your interest, making it more likely that you will retain the knowledge. You are able to learn at your own pace. And you may find that some skills you learn in one area are applicable in others, especially soft skills.

Cons: It can be easy to give in to distractions or become frustrated. If you are on a small team, it can also make you isolated from others. It can be hard to stay motivated.

Volunteering

Probably the most overlooked training opportunity is volunteering. There are lots of local organizations that can use all sorts of help. Believe it or not, if you are looking to break into the IT sector, you would do well to find a local group that could use some IT help. The easiest example that comes to mind is a church or a community center. Places that thrive on the assistance of volunteers need help in almost every area you can imagine.

And you do not need to feel that your volunteering has to be related to something technical. You could volunteer your time to mentor someone in your shop. Mentoring is a wonderful way to enhance your skills, especially your soft skills.

Pros: It is a great way to build your resume and get some actual experience. Classroom learning has a certain value, but real-world experience is always better. Plus, it is a great feeling to donate your time to helping others. In fact, you should do this regardless of the training opportunity.

Cons: The experience you get may be quite limited; chances are you will not be doing anything cutting edge. Unless you are mentoring someone else, you will most likely be working alone with little direction.

In-Service Training

This is also sometimes called a brown-bag lunch session. The idea is to offer training to employees by bringing in an outside trainer to conduct the class. Or a respected colleague might lead the instruction.

Pros: This is a good way to maximize your training dollars by bringing someone in house to conduct the training. If you are an employee being asked to train others, then it is also a great opportunity for you to learn even more. I have often told others that a good way to learn something is to try to teach it to others.

Cons: This creates time away from your desk, but not away from the office; you may find it difficult to focus on the training materials if you are needed to perform work duties. Materials may not always be on a topic you have interest in.

Professional Associations

You can find a professional association to suit your interests. Two that come to mind immediately are the Professional Association for SQL Server (PASS, http://sqlpass.org) and the Usability Professional's Association (UPA, `www.upassoc.org`). Both offer you the ability to participate in user group meetings and hold annual conferences.

Pros: Most will offer a basic membership at little or no cost. Membership status will typically include a newsletter that will alert you to upcoming events that allow for you to connect, share, and learn from others. Many of these events are free to attend.

Cons: There are not a lot of options as far as organized associations go, and you may be disappointed in the overall selection. Also, they may be nothing more than a networking focus as opposed to training or professional development. You will need to do extra research to find out the exact benefits of membership.

Continuing Education

A local college or university may offer a relevant class that could be of interest. Perhaps you are looking to get a degree in IT or maybe a more general MBA. Or you could just want to take one class in order to gain more knowledge on a particular subject.

Pros: Earn credits toward a degree. Classes are usually at night, meaning you do not lose any time from work. Classes typically run eight weeks unless they are part of a more formal degree or certification program.

Cons: Could be cost prohibitive; check with your HR department to see if your company has a policy on assisting with the costs of the classes. Classes are usually at night, meaning you lose time that could otherwise be spent with your family.

Classroom Training

Classroom training is any type of training that involves you or your colleagues having to go to a training center offsite and away from your office. In most cases this is going to cost some money, but there are also a lot of free events that are available. And by "free," I mean that you often have to sit through some sales pitches.

Pros: You'll receive very focused training on a particular subject area being taught by a professional trainer. Accompanying training materials are typically of high quality. You'll be encouraged to learn through the use of hands-on lab sessions (i.e., you get to learn by doing).

Cons: It can be cost prohibitive. It's difficult to judge the quality of the material until you are already in attendance. Given your level of work experience, you may find the classroom materials too easy, too advanced, too confusing, or impractical for your particular role in your shop.

Certifications

Certification is not a resource in and of itself; the training you receive from the sources just listed are the actual resources you will use (along with work experience) to earn the certification. Think of a certification as the end and the preceding resources as the means. And do not believe that certifications alone are going to be the easy path to fame and fortune.

> **TIP:** Certifications by themselves demonstrate very little. Certifications combined with work experience tell a more complete story.

Pros: Certification can greatly enhance your existing skills, and when combined with your experience, it can communicate your skill set to others.

Cons: It can be cast in a negative light, especially if you are long on certifications but short on experience. There are a *lot* of "brain dump" factories out there that offer shortcut methods to obtaining certifications; over time this can erode confidence in the value of the certification.

Building Your Case

You should now recognize the need for training and have some possible training resources listed. It should be quite easy for you to convince you manager that it is logical to send you to some training classes, right?

Wrong.

Never confuse logic with business intelligence. Your manager has a manager, most likely, and that manager is going to want some justification for spending training dollars on you no matter how big or small the expense. It will most likely fall to you to present a solid business case in order for you to secure this funding.

To go about building a solid business case for training, start by understanding what a business cares about most: revenue, expenses, and profit. As much as we all want to love our jobs and work in a happy, loving environment with unicorns and rainbows all around us, the fact is that money makes the world go round. If you want to secure the funding for training dollars, then you will need to demonstrate how the business will benefit by spending this money. If this sounds like I am saying, "It takes money to make money," that's because I am. But that's OK, because most corporations live by that very ideal; it will be up to you to show them how.

> **TIP:** The higher up you need to talk to someone about money, the more important it is you can demonstrate a financial return for any investment you are asking them to make on your behalf.

Here is a list of specific items to start gathering information about:

1. Determine your training needs.

2. Determine how many people need the training.

3. Determine which options will be used.

4. Calculate the associated costs/expenses.

5. Determine the benefits of training.

6. Determine the cost savings.

7. Measure your results!

Determine Your Training Needs

You will need to clearly identify your training needs, and they should align with a business goal or initiative in some way. For example, perhaps there is an effort to virtualize your database servers. You could list a training need for some aspect of virtualization. Or perhaps you want to learn about a particular tool and your company is also looking to build a data warehouse. If your training needs do not match any business needs, then you do not have training *needs*, you have training *wants*. And there is no reason for your company to simply give you what you want; there has to be a benefit for the company at some level.

Determine How Many People Need the Training

This will be important later on when you need to weigh your training options and calculate costs. There are times when you will find it easier to get training if you can also show that the training would benefit others as opposed to just yourself. Remember that you're always in competition for training dollars—your coworkers want that training money, too. You may have to justify your training budget by offering to train other employees upon your return. Besides, if only you go the training, then you might be the only person with the knowledge, and as a result you may find yourself in even more demand, which could easily erode your work/life balance (if it exists).

Determine Which Options Will Be Used

Review all the available training options listed previously and see which ones are viable. Which ones will suit your needs and accommodate everyone that needs to be trained? You may be able to mix and match a few options. Perhaps one person could attend a class, another could attend a conference, and someone else could find a side project to do some self-training on. Then the three of you can get together to connect, learn, and share from one another.

In our shop we tend to have each team member focus on one particular aspect of database administration. The other team members know who is focused on what, and leverage that knowledge when necessary. Over time we all become a little more knowledgeable in many different areas. This reduces the need to send us all to many different training sessions throughout the year.

Calculate the Associated Costs/Expenses

Start adding up everything you can think of with regard to costs. The easy costs to identify are the biggest ones, such as the cost of a class, a conference, or hiring a trainer to come onsite. Travel and lodging are also easy costs to identify when it comes to training expenses. Some of the hidden costs that are harder to identify are things like mileage on your car if you have to drive to a training center, or the purchase of prerequisite training materials such as books. And then there is your time away from the office, which you can express in the number of hours lost from work. If there are many people in the training class, you may find it easier to express this number in terms of a full-time equivalent (FTE).

> **TIP:** No expense is too small; write down everything you can possibly think of as an expense.

Try your best to think of every possible expense. You may not be able to cover everything, but you need your estimate to be as close to the final bill as possible.

Determine the Benefits of Training

Start by writing down every possible benefit you can think would be a result of the training. Do not limit yourself only to business-specific results as you may have done when listing out your training needs. Some of the benefits could be things like a reduction in turnover, fewer errors being made when using a system, or simply your ability to network with other professionals.

As you go down the list of the benefits, you should be able to divide them into two categories: those that can easily be shown to align with business goals and those that align to your personal goals. Take the personal goals and see if they can also be shown to have a business benefit.

For example, if you said that one of the benefits was your ability to network with other professionals, chances are your company will not care. But if you said, "I will be able to network with other professionals and that will allow for me to improve upon some necessary soft skills and will provide a benefit to the company in the future when I reach out to that network for help with technical issues," then your company may care a great deal.

Many of those personal goals you have listed can be shown to provide a business benefit; you just need to give it some thought.

Determine the Cost Savings

This can be difficult to calculate, as the benefits are not always going to be hard dollars. Most people typically focus on hard dollars and cost reductions that are easily calculated. It is fine to also look for training that will help with what is called "cost avoidance." This is where you save money that has not been spent yet.

An example of this would be virtualization. You may have some servers that are a few years old. You could either buy new hardware to replace the old servers, or you could look to virtualize the older hardware. The difference in costs between the physical and virtual environment would be considered cost avoidance.

> **TIP:** Understand the difference between a cost reduction and cost avoidance. You cannot claim to be saving your household millions of dollars a year by *not* buying diamonds, could you?

Cost savings can also be brought about by streamlining a process if you are able to quantify the amount of time saved as a result of the training. Another place to find cost savings is if you are able to take on an expanded role as a result of the training; perhaps you could start conducting future training classes and reduce the need for your company to hire an outside trainer.

Measure Your Results!

This last part may be the most important. After you put everything else together, take some time to think about how you will measure your success. If you have declared that there is cost savings then write down how you plan to calculate that savings once the training is complete. Same thing for cost avoidance; make certain you track everything you can with regard to the actual costs and the estimate costs had no training been given. All too often I see this part of any business case left out, as if measurements are either a forgotten component of any plan or that people just do not understand their importance.

Without measurements, you will not be able to validate the results of the training. If the results are less than expected, then you have the opportunity to learn from your experience and make corrections to future training plans. If the results are better than expected, then your measurements are going to be a valuable asset when you present your results to management.

I started this chapter by saying everyone always needs training. When your next round of training finishes, you need to keep track of how much you used that training over the year and how it's saved the business money. Doing so will make it easier for the business to send you to your next round of training and make you an even better employee.

Chapter 9

Connect. Learn. Share.

After you have established your routine and have become comfortable with your DBA skills, you may find yourself drawn toward helping others. Do not panic; it is perfectly natural to find yourself willing to help others. It is also natural to be timid when it comes to other database professionals and their skills. Every time I sit in a room of other DBA's I always assume everyone knows more than I do. Then I am surprised to find out that the people on the other side of the table are thinking the same thing about me.

One thing I have learned in my role as a DBA is that more often than not you are going to be able to find someone willing to help. Most DBA's I know are not afraid to say that they do not know something. This is in contrast to other professions where people tend to profess being an expert in something (TV talk-show hosts), or feel the need to pretend to be an expert, or don't want anyone to question their level of expertise at all (doctors or lawyers).

Because most DBA's are willing to admit they do not know something, most other DBA's are willing to help because they know that a time will come when they need some help as well.

TIP: No one person can know everything.

In this chapter, we will discuss the following:

1. Communications and how to get started (writing and speaking)

2. Professional associations

3. Networking basics

Communication

Communication skills are important for anyone regardless of their vocation. In today's wired world it is more important than ever to have strong communication skills. E-mail, blogs, phone calls, and face-to-face discussions are quite commonplace for most IT professionals. Individuals that have good communication skills have an advantage over those that lack those same communication skills.

> **TIP:** E-mail is a poor vehicle for communicating with others. Pick up the phone and talk with someone instead.

Often times, people tell me that when it comes to good communication skills they tend to think about people in positions of upper management. In other words, it is not something that they need to be concerned with at their particular level of employment. While it may be true that you need good communication skills in order to climb any corporate ladder, it is also true that good communication skills allow for you to maintain relationships with others around you. It is also true that most technology jobs advertised typically list "good communication skills" as a requirement.

If you already have good communication skills then it will be easier for you to connect, learn, and share with other professionals. If your communication skills need some work (and most people could always improve their communication skills to some degree), then there is only one way to get better: you need to practice. In my experience, the best way to get started is by doing all the things you want to improve.

Want to get better at talking on the phone? Talk on the phone more. Better at writing? Start by doing some extra reading and then doing some writing of your own. Want to get better at generating others' interest to buy into your ideas at meetings? Work on your posture and body language. But how and where do you get started with it all?

> **TIP:** Don't forget the clothes. Tom mentions posture and body language. Don't forget that those two items are a package wrapped in clothing. Think about what you wear to the office. Dress upwardly, within a zone of reasonableness. Every office has a high- and a low-end as to what is considered acceptable dress. Lean toward the high end. — Jonathan Gennick

Start Reading

For me, the best way to get started with communication skills was to start reading more. It did not matter what I was reading; it could be a book, a technical journal, a web site, a blog, or even a textbook. Over time I would start to find and identify with certain writing styles that made me want to read more. One of my favorite writers happens to be a blogger that got started by blogging about local sports teams. He is now one of the most well-known writers for a major sports network's web site. His writing style was so natural and seemingly so effortless that it made me more comfortable with the idea of writing for myself.

As I fell into being a DBA, I had less time to read about sports and was spending more time reading technical web sites, blogs, and articles. The more I read, the more I started to find which writing styles were most appealing for me. This became important later on as I searched for my own particular writing style.

Reading allows for you to connect with, and learn from, the author. The more you read, the more you will be drawn to certain writers, and the more you will be connected to your community as a whole. For example, you may subscribe to several blogs, all written by some of the prominent leaders in your industry. By reading their blogs, or other trade publications, you can get a sense of what others in your field are doing. You can see how they have solved certain issues, or read about their reviews of a product, and get a sense of sharing some common ground.

One day you will find yourself reading some article that describes a solution to a problem that is similar to something you have seen recently. You will suddenly think to yourself *"Hey, what if I took their solution and see if it would work for me here?"* You'll make a few changes and deploy the solution to see if it is what you need, which will increase that connection you feel with the author, and also have learned something in the process.

Therefore, reading more also has a residual benefit in addition to helping your communication skills; you get to improve your technical skills (or whatever you are reading about) as well. As your skills improve to a certain level, you will start to think about attending training seminars, lectures, code camps, or conferences.

Start Attending

Reading can trigger something inside of you to want to get more details than what a book will provide. This will lead you to look at attending events in person. Such an event could be a conference, a training class or seminar, a user group meeting, or a lecture somewhere.

Most of us have attended lectures for years while in high school and college. When I was in graduate school we also had colloquium, which are seminars that are open to the public. Think of a user group meeting except without the vendor and free pizza. There are lots of opportunities for you to attend a lecture being given by someone else. Attending such functions allows you the possibility to connect, learn, and share with the speaker and others.

> **TIP:** Even half-day events are worthwhile. Make a point to attend and meet new people.

I still recall the very first session I attended at a conference. I remember watching this person present a talk on query plans and I was thinking to myself:

> *"I used to give better talks when describing how to find the area of an ellipse to my Math-107 students in grad school. If this guy can present here, maybe I could as well."*

Now, to be fair, his talk was not bad, it just made me understand that by that point in my life I had already spent a lot of time in front of an audience, and that I could do technical presentations as long as I was prepared. I could not roll into a technical talk as if it was an algebra class, I would bomb.

Attending functions will also allow for you to get an idea of what works well when presenting and what doesn't work well. This will be valuable information for you when you want to start thinking about how you would go about giving your own presentation. Will your talk need a lot of demos? Perhaps more pictures and fewer words would work better?

Before you can think about speaking in front of others you will need to be able to write down your thoughts coherently. And the only way to get better at writing is by writing, of course.

JOIN A FORUM

By Jared Still

Also consider joining a forum, mailing list, or some other venue by which other technical professionals can pose technical problems that they have been unable to solve. An active forum is like a perpetual conference. Be active too. Plus you can't help but meet new people as you learn.

Start Writing

I was never a writer. In fact, I became a math major because I did not have to write. As an undergrad, I would drop classes that required a term paper and take a math class simply because there was no writing involved. I still remember how excited I was to have gotten a seat in a class titled "Abnormal Psychology" and the disappointment I felt when on the first day the professor explained that I was going to write a ten page paper at the end of the semester. I left the class, walked over to the registrar, and switched into a class called "Numerical Analysis."

When I went to graduate school my world was turned upside down. In my very first class, the professor explained that my homework was to be written out, in words, and submitted. So, I could not even write a "2," I needed to spell it out as "two." Simple mathematical statements and formulas became sentences and paragraphs. It was pure sadistic torture. I honestly did not think I would make it through. The professor explained that I needed to improve my reading and writing if I was going to have any future as a mathematician, or anything else.

And, she was right.

That was the beginning of my current writing skills, to be honest, right there in graduate school while learning some linear algebra. In the years following graduate school, I would find it necessary to do a bit of writing from time to time in my job as a programmer. I doubt anything I wrote at that time is worth much of a read these days, except for a laugh. No, the real first things I wrote about were quite personal.

My wife and I had our first child. I decided to put up a family blog where I could write about everything and post pictures of the baby so that people could view them whenever they wanted. I blogged two or three times a month right up until we had our second child the following year. Then I was blogging for both of them, and I continue to do so to this day. I was able to start writing because there was something passionate for me to write about. Over time, I also realized I had a passion for technical things as well, so I started blogging for myself as a professional in addition to the family blog. The fact that I had found all these things that I loved, and that I loved to write about them, made it very easy for the words to leave my fingers.

The years of reading made it easier for me to understand that I wanted my own voice, my style, and to become a writer. Having something passionate to write about made it even easier. If you want to get better as a writer then you need to write more, and the easiest way to write more is to find something you love to write about.

> **TIP:** When you have a passion for doing something then it feels less like work, and it will actually energize you to achieve more.

I would encourage anyone looking to become a better communicator to start writing, perhaps by posting to their own blog. Do not assume blogging means that you think people care about what you have to say. They don't, trust me. No, you need to think of blogging as a way for you to get better as a writer. Over time, you will think about writing something to be published on a web site somewhere. This will be your chance to share your experience with others, to connect with them, and help someone else learn something new.

Gradually, after all that writing, you are going to want to talk to someone about it.

FIND QUESTIONS. DO RESEARCH. WRITE.

By Jared Still

A good way to get started writing is to find a question that you don't know the answer to. Research the problem. When you feel you have something worthwhile to contribute, propose a solution. You can write your findings in a forum or as a blog entry. Go with whichever medium leaves you feeling the most comfortable.

Don't be too modest. Anyone who does some research and already has some knowledge of the technology in question can make a worthwhile contribution. You'll learn something new, and your efforts will likely improve your social networking as well.

Start Speaking

I have been in positions of leadership since I was 18 years old. As such, I have been standing in front of groups of people and making speeches for a long time now. However, each time I speak in front of others I get nervous. I still remember how nervous I was to teach algebra while a graduate student, and it certainly was not because I was unfamiliar with the material or that I thought someone in the audience knew more about binomials than I did.

Once I was at a conference where a good friend was presenting. She was nervous a little bit but she told me that in order to get better at public speaking she started singing karaoke because if you can sing in front of strangers then speaking is easy. I can agree to that; but you won't find me singing in a bar anytime soon. For me the only way to combat the nervousness is to simply get started. Once I get going it gets a little easier. What really makes me feel better is when I can interact with someone in the audience. Lots of times before I get started I will find someone in the first few rows to chat with while others are taking their seats. It sets me at ease and allows for me to warm up a bit.

> **TIP:** Always take the time to get warmed up before you present your session, it will enhance the quality of your presentation.

Another way to set yourself, and your audience, at ease is to tell stories during your presentation. You have probably heard about people saying that you should start off your talk with a joke in order to help relax everyone, including yourself. What I have found is often the best speakers are the ones that have anecdotal stories spread throughout their presentation. Storytelling is a powerful way to get a message across to hundreds of people at the same time.

Now, not everyone needs to be able to make speeches to hundreds of people. I think the most people I have ever spoken to at one time would be less than two hundred. The number of people present at the talk really does not matter to me, what matters most is the audience and my material. That is why it is important for me to connect with the audience as soon as possible. Doing so will make it easier for me to share my information with them and hopefully for them to learn as well.

My first technical presentation was at a local user group. I used the feedback from the group to prep for a presentation at a national conference later that same year. Since then, I have spoken dozens of times in various formats. One thing I have found to be true is that most people relate to storytelling or anecdotal stories better than to a straightforward technical discussion. I strive to be a good storyteller, but I am nowhere near as good as I hope to be someday. That is why I continue to present, because I want to keep getting better.

The reason I want to get better is not because I want to keep giving talks at conferences. I want to get better so that I can give talks to my peers anywhere. Even more important are those times when I need to give talks to upper management. I want to be able to give my talk with confidence, just as someone with good communication skills would. That means I need to practice speaking, which means I need to do more writing, attend more functions, and do more reading.

They all work together in order to make you a better communicator.

GETTING PAST THE FEAR

By Jonathan Gennick

Tom's friend used karaoke to increase her confidence in public speaking. For me, what helped a lot was working with a youth group.

I was so terrified at public speaking early in my career that I would flatly refuse any request to speak in front of people. Then one day I got roped into helping with a youth group at my church. I don't clearly recall just how that came about, but suddenly there I was, in front of over a dozen teens and pre-teens who would laugh, jeer, and happily tell me anytime I was boring.

Adults are so polite by comparison. I still get nervous sometimes, and I'm not the best presenter, but the fear is gone. When I get nervous now, it's the healthy sort of nervousness that comes from being anxious that everything go according to plan. Gone is the cold ball of panic-inducing fear that used to slam into me at the thought of speaking in front of a group.

Professional Associations

Years ago I had the opportunity to attend a conference for a professional association. Until then, I had always thought of conferences as a place where people go to sit in a room and listen to lectures. The first sign I had that there was more to a conference was when I saw the vendors and their exhibits. I started to understand that there was more than just attending some boring lectures; there was a real energy at this event. People were not just learning; *they were connecting*.

The conference was being put on by a professional association. My only knowledge of professional associations at that time was my being a member of a couple while in graduate school. Every student was enrolled in a couple of associations by default. That meant we got a monthly newsletter in our mailbox and that was about it. The only other members I knew were my fellow students.

During this conference, I began to understand more about the benefits of joining a professional association. Being a member allowed people the opportunity to keep up to date on the latest trends in their industry. They were afforded endless networking opportunities; connecting, learning, and sharing with many other like-minded individuals.

> **TIP:** There is great strength in numbers; being a member of a professional association can give you great strength.

After I became a database administrator, I went to my first conference. It was put on by the Professional Association for SQL Server (PASS). I was determined to take in all the benefits of membership possible. I wanted to become the best DBA that I could be, and I knew that one way to achieve that goal was to join a professional association.

On the first day of the conference, I met two people that have remained close colleagues to this day. Following the conference I remained in touch with these two individuals and we were able to help each other from time to time. Not just when issues arose, but also for very general questions regarding best practices. When we did not have answers for each other, we did our best to help point each other in the right direction.

By the time I attended my third PASS conference, I had a network of roughly 30 people that I could rely on for similar help. I was also surprised that the more experience I got then the more I was able to help others. Soon enough I found myself starting to write articles for publication as I wanted to share my experiences with others. There is no doubt that I have personally grown as a database professional simply by becoming a member of PASS.

Through the years my involvement with PASS has given me chances to speak and to write. More importantly, it has given me the chance to meet others. I like to stress to people the fact that PASS is an *association* of database professionals. I often get asked the question "Why should I bother joining any professional association?" Following are the answers I often give.

Latest Trade Information

Being a member of a professional association allows for you to stay informed about the latest in industry trends. Sure, you could hope to get the latest information from web sites, blogs, and magazines. However, when you are a member you tend to get access to information *before* it ends up in print. This kind of insider access can be invaluable when you are architecting your environment.

Membership allows for more than just cutting edge information on industry trends. You also get information on products and services specific to your industry. Typically vendors will target a professional association and their members when it comes to their products. Nowhere is this more evident than at a conference. You will see dozens of vendors lined up to show you their products in the hopes that they can earn your business. This allows for you to get an idea for lots of products and how they could be applicable for your shop.

Still another advantage would be the ability to exchange information with other members regarding processes; in other words, ask "How do you do this in your shop?" You will find that many members are willing to help other members by sharing their experiences.

Writing Opportunities

Most professional associations offer some type of publication. It could be a web site, a newsletter in the form of an e-mail, or a printed journal. It does not really matter as to the type and form of communication used; each is an opportunity for you to write and be published. The more you write and get published the more name recognition you will build over time.

> **TIP:** Yes, writing opportunities would include a book, believe it or not.

You may soon find yourself being offered additional writing opportunities. Remember all those vendors that target professional associations? Well, they like to have people write articles, tech briefs, and white papers. There may even be the chance for you to collaborate on a book (or even write your very own).

Speaking Opportunities

Many professional associations have annual meetings or conferences. By being a member you increase your chances of securing a speaking opportunity. Some associations also have local meetings that are less informal but still offer you an opportunity to participate by speaking. You may not always need to be a member in order to speak, but it certainly never hurts your chances.

There is also the chance that you could find speaking opportunities simply by responding to advertisements in trade publications or journals. It is possible that a company or organization could be looking for someone with specialization. They may contact your association in order to find someone willing to speak on a particular subject. I have often seen this done when a company is looking for someone to conduct some training, but I have also seen it done by companies looking to put together a larger one day event.

Networking

You certainly do not need to join a professional association if you want to do some networking. But if you were to get started in networking, would it not make sense to network with others in your industry? Why spend time networking with other professionals outside your field?

In addition to networking with other professionals in your particular field, you will be able to network with vendors, which can be quite valuable especially when you need some quick support.

Of course, one of the biggest advantages to networking is the career opportunities that can arise as a result. You never know when a job will open up; it is nice when you are the first person that someone thinks of when an opportunity arises.

Networking can be hard to understand and even harder to get started. Let's review some of the basics of networking in order to help you get started.

Networking Basics

I know more than a handful of people that think of networking as a dirty word. Being a shy person I find it difficult to get accustomed to networking as much as anyone else. I do, however, understand the value in building a wide network and how it allows you to connect, learn, and share with others. Still many people seem to understand the real purpose of networking.

The purpose of networking is to build a series of mutually beneficial relationships.

Seriously, it is that simple. The whole idea of creating a network is to build relationships that benefit both parties. Sometimes you will need help from your network. Other times, you will be able to help others in your network. Plus, the more help you give to people in your network the more help you are likely to receive in return.

> **TIP:** Think of your career as a ship, and your network as your crew. If you want to sail far, then you need a reliable crew. The larger your ship, the larger your network needs to be.

But how does someone go about building such a network? It is certainly not an easy thing to do for most people. Meeting new people when you are in a room full of individuals that all seem to be interacting nicely with each other is not something that comes naturally for many. It can seem rather overwhelming to meet strangers.

Building Your Network

To build your network you will need to meet other people. There is really no other way; you simply have to interact with others. This can be done through either a physical interaction (say, a networking event) or through what is called social networking. Social networking involves web sites that specialize in your ability to interact with others in online forums. Some of the more well-known social networking sites are Twitter, Facebook, and LinkedIn.

Many people find it easier to interact socially online with strangers than if they were to interact physically with others in a group setting. Even in situations that are not necessarily a networking event some people find it awkward to talk to strangers. Consider the following scenario:

> *John was in need of buying a replacement headlight for his car. John was not mechanically inclined in any way and typically he would just go to the dealer for any type of repair. This time he decided that he was going to try to fix something for himself because others had told him how satisfying it was to do so.*

John was not comfortable when he entered the store and tried to blend in with the other customers. He looked around for a headlight but could not find one. He was afraid to ask for help because he did not want anyone to know that he could not find something as simple as a headlight. At one point, he found a young man in a store uniform and asked him for help, but the young man was not very helpful.

Frustrated, John heads over to the customer service desk to finally ask for some help. "Can someone please show me where the car headlights are?"

The man behind the desk asked John, "Sir, have you ever shopped for car parts before?"

"No," John replied, "this is my first time. How did you know?"

"Sir," the man replied, "this is a pool supply store."

If you want to build your network then you are going to need to do two very important things. First, you are going to have to interact with others, in some way. Second, you have to make certain you are in the right room to begin with.

Feeling Comfortable

So how do you get past those feelings that make you uncomfortable?

Find out what things make you most uncomfortable, and then don't do those things.

Sounds simple, right? Well, it depends.

First, it could be difficult to ascertain what it is that makes you most uncomfortable. I know some people that are afraid of talking with new people because they are concerned that they may make a bad impression. I know others that are afraid of new people because they are not comfortable with themselves to start with. You need to find out *exactly* what your biggest concern is with meeting new people. Doing so will give you the opportunity to overcome those challenges, which also happens to be the second difficulty you face.

Most people find it uncomfortable to attend events where they do not already know someone. If that also describes yourself then make an effort to find a friend to attend the event with you. Just make certain you do not spend all night talking with your friend and you never meet anyone new.

TIP: It always helps to have a conversation starter. If you cannot think of anything else, you can always start with the weather.

Another tip that helps many people is to arrive early. That way it is easier to start a conversation with someone else that arrives early. If you arrive fashionably late you may find it more difficult to inject yourself into a conversation taking place among a group of people. When you arrive early you can not only talk with some of the other few early arrivals, you may also find it easier to move from your current group to another group.

This is one reason why some people prefer social networking. It is more comfortable to meet people online than in person. I would remind you, however, that you are not anonymous when online. Be mindful of whatever comments you post to these forums.

How to Approach Others

I am not a natural conversationalist by any means. Walking up to strangers and talking to them is just not something I am very comfortable with. I have, however, learned a few things over the years that helps me understand how and when to approach others during a networking or social events.

The first thing to notice is how people are interacting with each other. No matter how many people in a group, that group is always considered either open or closed.

An open group means that people's body positions are such that they are inviting others to join in their conversation. When people are standing and talking they will naturally position their bodies in a specific way depending on the nature of the discussion. Most discussions lend themselves to the group being open.

A closed group is formed when the nature of the conversation is such that the participants are turned toward each other in a manner that is not inviting. This is a group that you would not want to try to interject yourself into a conversation, you would want to scan the room and look for open groups instead.

> **TIP:** I like to look for people that are looking for people. Hopefully that makes sense. In other words, often times there are people who have that inviting look, a look that says come talk to me or I wish someone was talking to me. —Sylvester Carstarphen

Once you have figured out which groups are open, you will need to go over and introduce yourself. It does not have to be anything fancy or difficult. Just a simple, "Hello, my name is Tom, nice to meet you." is all you need. Well, you should use your own name, of course. After that you can get a conversation started with a basic question such as "How did you hear about this event?" or "What do you do for work?" You could even make a statement, like "I am nervous." or "I have trouble meeting new people." are all acceptable conversation starters.

After you have spent some time, you may want to move on to a new group. There is no hard and fast rule on the amount of time that must be spent with any one group. But you will need to have an exit strategy in place before leaving your group for another. Do not be so rude that you would leave a person by themselves, of course, but it is perfectly acceptable to simply say "excuse me" and move to another part of the room. Yes, it really is that simple.

One of my favorite parts of these types of events is the power you have when connecting others. You may spend five minutes with one group and learn a few things about a person. Then, twenty minutes later, you may find someone new that has something in common with that other person you had met earlier. So you take the time to introduce those two people together.

Why would you want to do this? Remember that you are all looking to build mutually beneficial relationships. If you can connect two people that may be able to help each other then you are helping others to build their networks. You can be certain that those two people are going to remember you as the person that introduced them to each other. Chances are they will return the favor by introducing you to someone that shares common interests with yourself.

There is real power in being the person that helps to connect others.

Choosing the Right Room

Where are some good places to go when you are looking for networking? Well, I have already talked about the value of professional associations. If you attend events sponsored by your professional association, you would at least know that others attending the event are people in the same field or industry as yourself. That could make conversations a little easier. Some common places to meet others would be conferences, user groups, local events, and training seminars.

If you want to build a mutually beneficial relationship with someone else then you need to make certain that you both have something of value and interest to each other. It makes little sense to be shopping for car headlights in a pool supply store, so why would you network in a room filled with people outside your profession or field of interest? However, I see and hear about this exact situation from people that tell me how disappointed they are with networking events.

Make certain you are in the right room to begin with before complaining about how bad your results are.

Making It Easier

I often hear about how hard networking can be. While I like to remind people that most things in life that are worthwhile are also sometimes difficult, I am also one of those that likes to have things made easy. One way to make networking easy is to know what your goals are. If you are looking to increase sales then you are going to want to find a specific type of room to network. If you are looking to simply increase your number of professional contacts then you are going to want a different type of room. The last thing you want to do is invest time and energy into a networking effort only to find that you are in the wrong room.

Another way to make networking easier is to simply have good manners. If you can talk (and chances are you have been talking since you were very young) and you have good manners, then you will be surprised at how easy networking can be. Remember how you can leave a group by simply saying "excuse me." Well, that is just good manners, and people that demonstrate good manners often stand out, are well liked, and respected.

Successful networking requires some work and effort, yet a lot of that work and effort end up becoming helpful habits. Before you know it, you will be a natural at networking.

Chapter 10

Summary

I still remember walking into that classroom at Washington State University. I was a graduate student and Teaching Assistant and was about to teach my very first pre-calculus class. I had never been a teacher before (except as a substitute) and really had no idea what to expect. We had been given some training in the days before classes were to begin, but nothing could have prepared me completely for what I was to experience. The training consisted mostly of practicing some basic lectures in front of our peers. I do not recall there being a lot of formal instruction written down, it was mostly group discussions.

Likewise, I still remember the first days that I took over as the database administrator. Any time anything went wrong with the mystery that is a database, I was called upon to provide an immediate answer. If I didn't have the answer, I was expected to stay at my desk until one could be found. Well, OK, that was the pressure I put upon myself because I was foolish enough to think that each and every database administrator already knew everything there is to know. Yes, I was that foolish.

How I wish that someone could have handed me a book that would outline what to expect over the coming weeks, months, and years; a book that would help me to be successful as a database administrator and outline my career growth from day one.

That is why I wrote this book. I wanted to write a book that I wish someone would have written and handed to me on my first day. I have been a database administrator for over six years now, but the learning curve during those first two was steep. I always seemed to be behind, always reacting to a situation or need, and rarely finding time to be proactive. Over time, I learned how to get ahead and I hope that the information in the preceding chapters allows for you to do the same.

Getting There

How you got here does not matter. What you do from your first day forward is how you will be measured. No one is going to be concerned about your past, all they will want are tangible results delivered with a ribbon on top. People from all walks of life become database administrators; very few people grow up with the idea in their mind that they will be a DBA.

Sometimes, however, people just know they want to get involved in database administration. That was certainly the case for me. Most others tend to fall into the role by accident. They find themselves doing a few administrative tasks here and there, and before they know it they are doing more and more. You will find that there are many paths to becoming a DBA. Getting there can be seen as either an impossible journey or as a journey you did not even know was happening.

If you are looking to become a DBA and feel as if you are not being given an opportunity, then you need to take matters into your own hands. Start finding opportunities to get yourself the necessary skills. There is a wealth of free training available online these days. There is also plenty of training available for a fee. I would always advise anyone to get as much hands-on experience as possible, in addition to any training offered through books and manuals. Plus you can always donate your time to local organizations in order to get that hands-on experience.

If you truly want to become a DBA, there are many ways to get there. Some paths may take longer than others, so you need to remain positive and keep visualizing the end result.

Being There

Getting to become a DBA may seem daunting at times. Once you find yourself in the role that you had been visualizing you may find yourself overwhelmed from time to time. Even seasoned database administrators can find themselves feeling overwhelmed by the volume of tasks at their fingertips. You may not be able to avoid being in over your head on any given day, but there are things you can do to keep those days to a minimum.

First off, you need to lay a solid foundation. One of the best ways to do this is by documenting as much as possible. Write down everything you can, no matter how important it may (or may not) seem at the time. The documentation will serve you well, as learning by wrote is a great way to memorize information.

Second, after you begin documenting everything you can find, you can then share your knowledge and experiences with your coworkers. Find ways to increase the flow of communication between all the teams in your shop. Got Sharepoint? Build yourself a portal and use it to publish useful information. You can even use it to publish T-SQL tips and tricks, or to discuss some basics of database design. Over time, you will find out what forms of communication work best for everyone in your shop.

Staying There

Getting there can be tough. Being there can be tougher. And staying there can be the hardest thing of all. If you want to stay, then you will need to move beyond the technical skills and start working on the soft skills.

Schedule times to meet with others, even if it is just a phone call to someone in a different office. Manage as many relationships as best as you can, keeping in mind that different people will need to be treated, well, differently. Find out what information they want or need from you and look to find ways to provide that information on a regular basis.

> **TIP:** Don't isolate yourself. If most of your work is done solo, find ways to collaborate with others in IT, users, and colleagues in your social network. No one is an island. We all need to work with others. Doing so will help you appreciate what others are doing, and make you more visible for the work that you do. —Jared Still

Another way to make sure you stick around for a while is to continue your professional development. Look to supplement your working tasks with some training tasks as you will always need to stay ahead of the curve. Download and install CTP's whenever possible. And read. You will need to read a lot. Stay on top of latest industry trends and communicate those trends to your peers. Engage others in discussions that are more about design and architecture and less about production issues.

However, do take time for yourself. Put your family first whenever possible. But remain responsive and responsible, and never be afraid to admit that you do not know everything.

You spent a long time getting here, so make certain you are enjoying your life and your career.

Index